This book is dedicated to every contrarian, nonconformist, black sheep, heretic, misfit, and weirdo.

IT'S TIME TO QUESTION HOW CHRISTIANS BELIEVE

IT'S TIME TO QUESTION

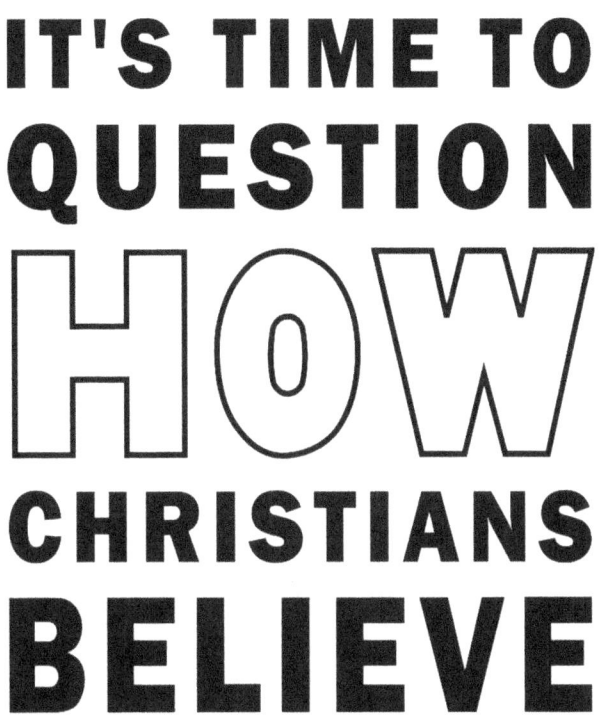

CHRISTIANS BELIEVE

**INSTEAD OF ANOTHER DEBATE
ABOUT WHAT CHRISTIANS BELIEVE**

Luther R. Palmer III, Ph.D.

www.LutherPalmerPhD.com
@LutherPalmerPhD

LuPalm
Wonders
Publishing

Dayton, Ohio

Contents

Preface

In September of 2021, a Florida man drove 20 miles to a home he had never been to before and told a woman he had never met before that God wanted him to speak to her daughter. She wisely refused his request, and he left, but he returned later that evening and killed the woman and her entire family. He did this one week after attending a church service for the first time in several years, and then telling his girlfriend that he could communicate directly with God. Hearing this incredibly sad story motivated me to finally finish this book, not because of *what* this man did, but because of the role that Christianity's problematic *how* played.

I had been tinkering with the book for years and putting the finishing touches on it for several months. This book was difficult to write from the very beginning, not only because I'm a slow and methodical writer, but also because I was never supposed to be an Atheist. I come from two large Christian families full of preachers, Christian educators, gospel singers, and other church leaders. I thought Atheists were just mad at God and had simply decided to stop praying and going to church. Actually disbelieving in God's entire existence was completely unfathomable, but then it happened to me. It felt liberating on an intellectual level, but also a little isolating socially. I wanted to write a letter to my family explaining what happened and why, and this book was born out of the process I went through to write that letter.

I knew my parents would be heartbroken, so I wanted to write compassionately about this belief system they still valued. I did not want to insult them or any others who would read the letter. I also wanted to be intellectually honest, meaning I didn't want to misrepresent Christianity in any way, just to make it an easier target for criticism. I wanted everything I said about Christianity to be true, which is made difficult by the fact that there are so many different variations of the faith, often directly conflicting with each other. Lastly, I wanted to be succinct and clear, which is difficult, but it pushed me to dig down to the fundamental roots of my decision to leave.

Unlike so many others who have walked away from Christianity, my story doesn't include any personal trauma, abuse, or the untimely death of a loved one. When I started writing the letter, I had several significant issues with Christianity itself, not in connection with any specific individuals, groups, or difficult life experiences. I started by writing about each of my objections individually. I wrote about my challenges with the Bible and how Christians use it. Then I wrote about the problems with prayer, then prophecy, spiritual discernment, miracles, and even faith. What started as a letter had become a set of personal notes that helped me organize and clarify my thoughts. But as I began to compare my objections to each individual aspect of Christianity, I noticed a common vulnerability to them all – *how*.

The subjective and vulnerable *how* of Christianity is what drove me away, and I decided to write this book when I realized how dangerous, pervasive, and yet undeniable this aspect of Christianity is. This is not just a book for Atheists and others who are already very critical of Christianity, though. I sincerely hope that stalwart Christians will also read this book, recognize the vulnerability of Christianity's *how*, and then work toward less subjective tools to support their behaviors and beliefs. At minimum, I hope it leads believers to seek communities and leaders who approach their beliefs with humility, and who are less dogmatic and punitive. I would also be happy to learn that someone regarded their own spiritual journey with more grace after reading here how difficult it can be to find clarity and assurance within Christianity.

I do not intend for this book to be an attack on Christianity, as Christianity is merely a symptom, not the root cause. Even if Christianity were eradicated, the underlying issue – *how* these beliefs were constructed – would persist and continue to be exploited in the formation of other beliefs. The real issue lies in the *how* of belief, and that is what I aim to address here. This is why adherents of other faiths will recognize similar vulnerabilities in the *how* of their own beliefs.

I included here next the actual letter I gave to my immediate family. And then after a brief introduction, the notes I wrote are stacked into this book as chapters. Some of these notes are about aspects of the Christian *how*, such as miracles and prophecy, and other notes are about topics such as the problem with subjectivity and the perceived value of Christianity. Near the end of the book, I answer some of the questions Christians typically ask me, which provides some insight into how I now find purpose, pursue morality, and have hope for the future. This is The Alternative chapter.

Interspersed throughout the book, I share snippets of my personal deconversion story. Walking away from Christianity wasn't an overnight decision – it was a gradual process shaped by a few pivotal insights and experiences. Moments like the David Koresh standoff in Waco, Texas, and the birth of one of my daughters didn't just change how I viewed Christianity; they changed how I viewed myself. If I was more clever, I would have correlated each snippet with the content in the preceding or following chapter. But that didn't happen, so they're presented in chronological order.

After an "appeal" that also serves as a conclusion, I created an Appendix in which I share some of my favorite quotes about Atheism, Christianity, science, faith, and belief. I started compiling these quotes several years ago, and this seemed like a great place to put them for other lovers of thought-centered and thought-provoking quotes.

A final note – I often refer to Jesus Christ, God the Father, and the Holy Spirit collectively as the Christian god. I learned that "God" should always be capitalized as a proper noun, and I do not mean the uncapitalized "god" to be an insult, but more-so the placement of the Christian god in proper context with the many other gods humans revere. This is similar to the usage of the proper noun Sun as a name for our sun. When we talk about other suns, and even our sun, the word isn't always a proper noun and is not always capitalized. I also refer to the Christian god using masculine pronouns, as Christian Bibles do, although it may be valuable for us all to abandon this practice.

A second final note – The book cover shows many different representations of Jesus, in a nod to the notion that humans can create God in their own image. These images were created using artificial intelligence (AI), and are the only AI-generated content in this book.

The Letter

Family,

I could not have had a better experience as a Christian. Both sides of my family having multi-generational heritage in Seventh-Day Adventist Christianity provided me with an unambiguous spiritual pathway, and a sense of community and connection to both sides of my extended families. I grew up with cousins, second cousins, and third cousins who were all Christian. Family reunions were highlighted with an amazing church service with powerful singing and piercing sermons. People were baptized and babies were blessed.

Our immediate family attended church every week, and financial sacrifices were made to send me to good Christian schools. I found Seventh-Day Adventism to be a relatively conservative form of Christianity, but I never felt oppressed by the religion. I was baptized into the faith at nine years old and would later preach a few mediocre sermons at my church and Christian schools.

I attended Oakwood University, the only Black Seventh-Day Adventist Christian university in the United States, and received a great education. On Saturday mornings at

Oakwood, the entire dormitory ironed clothes and played gospel music while getting ready for church. Weekly chapels, courses on Christian Education and the Life and Teachings of Jesus Christ were required of all students at Oakwood. I ultimately married a Christian woman, and we were all set to live happily ever Christian.

I lead with this description of my overall happiness being raised as a Christian because what follows is a critique of the Christian faith, and I don't want anyone to think this comes from a place of resentment toward organized religion, or because of any ill feelings about Christians themselves or how they treated me. It is true that many people who walk away from Christianity have had awful experiences with professed Christians, and now they can only see God through the lens of these interactions. But this is not the case for me, as my experiences with Christians have been nearly all positive. I also avoided the pull of legalism within Christianity. I believed the Ten Commandments were guidelines provided for our benefit, and that central to the life of a Christian is a personal relationship with Jesus Christ. Although I was never the most church going or outwardly spiritual person in my adulthood, I actively pursued a relationship with Jesus Christ and desired to be more like him.

I have chosen to walk away from the entirety of Christianity, not just a particular denomination or brand. It can sometimes be counterproductive to discuss "Christianity" because so many individuals operate within their own variation of the religion. Although the label carries with it an assumed association to organized religion, there is no such requirement. Christians may switch between denominations and churches as often as they choose, or they may abandon church altogether. My problems with Christianity rise above its people and its doctrines, and rest squarely on the shoulders of the supposed architect of this way of life. I am walking away from the idea of Jesus Christ, and hence any desire to follow him.

I am an Atheist.

This will come as a great surprise to many of you who only interact with me occasionally, and may be no surprise at all to others. Some of you have witnessed me questioning and challenging Christianity, quite obnoxiously at times, and have heard or read my lack of satisfaction with the available explanations or rationales. No, I cannot prove that God doesn't exist. In fact, I make no claim about whether he exists or not, but I choose to live my life as if he does not. This is a different understanding of Atheism than I once had, but most of the atheists I've encountered would be more than happy to accept the existence of God if any objective evidence became available. In the meantime, the likelihood the Christian god exists is no greater than for the existence of Vishnu, Mahavira, Zeus, or Osiris, and I am just as atheistic about the Christian god as Christians are about these other gods.

My primary objection to Christianity is its reliance on the subjective nature of personal experiences to determine what is right, wrong, or real, and the associated certainty that these experiences are influenced by a resurrected man-god who created the universe. I do not object to what Jesus said as much as I object to how Christians have come to accept that this god is real and all others are not, and that this god is all knowing, perfect in character, and worthy of their fully surrendered will. I do believe people experience things that cannot be explained given our current understanding of consciousness, medicine, and astronomy. I will never dispute anyone's experiences or feelings, but I now disagree that the only or most useful explanation for these experiences is the workings of a supernatural being.

The kindest and most compassionate Christian of all time and the cruelest and most insensitive Christian don't just agree that Jesus Christ was the literal son of God. They also agree in the efficacy of our personal experiences to reveal to us who God is and what he wants us to be doing. Yet these two individuals would regard each other as the best examples of how vulnerable our understanding of these experiences are to our own biases, traditions, desires, fears, and other social influences. Human emotions and feelings are powerful enough to make us see, hear, and feel things that do not exist, so an invisible, inaudible, and intangible god can be *seen* doing whatever we want him to be doing, which then allows us to mold his character into whatever we want it to be. Anyone can elevate their own ideals and morality onto a deity, and then claim it to be unimpeachable. This is why so many versions of God are being worshiped within Christianity today. By professing that faith is the most virtuous pathway to truth, even above more objective approaches such as evidence and reason, Christianity encourages a dangerous connection between the frailty of our subjective biases and the authority of an irreproachable deity. Invisible and inaudible gods can never be eradicated, because they are us, and are born out of our own desire to be right and authoritative.

It seems obvious to me now that we make gods in our image. It has taken a while, but I now see that kind people worship kind gods, and vindictive people worship vindictive gods. The gods we serve feel like mirrors of our own morality, so I no longer listen or look out for messages from Jesus Christ or a holy spirit. I do not pray. I do not interpret unexplainable phenomena as miraculous. I do not read the Bible in search of moral guidance, or regard the book as divinely inspired. I do not look forward to the second coming and an eternity with risen loved ones.

All throughout my life as I had been becoming Christian, I was also maturing, growing, and seeing more of the world. I was becoming a skeptic, procrastinator, perfectionist, conspiracy theorist, debater, contrarian, glass-is-half-full guy, absent-minded professor and so much more. I was becoming myself in the sense that I did not always understand these aspects of my personality and how they manifest themselves in my feelings and decision making. I didn't always know how to corral these parts of myself and use them for my benefit, and still too often fail at it. I'm still learning about myself and still changing, but I've settled on a view of myself that feels like a healthy mix of the person who others see me to be, the person who my emotions and actions suggest I am, and the person I am internally working to become.

That being said, I no longer see a role for Christianity in my life. I no longer feel benefited by Christianity, as it became increasingly difficult to figure out and defend what I was supposed to believe and then apply those beliefs to help me navigate this world. This was a difficult reality to accept because so much of my family's interaction is rooted in the idea of a shared faith. But meeting people from other cultures and religious backgrounds has broadened my perspective and allows me to more easily disentangle my own personal experiences, and those of my family, from what is happening in the world. Christianity and the Christian experience now seem rather ordinary. People share the same limitations and capacities for joy, kindness, love, pride, jealousy, and greed, regardless of whether they acknowledge the Christian god, no god at all, or any of the thousands of other gods. This was perhaps the most damning realization I had about

Christianity, since I could be persuaded to continue in a tradition I didn't fully understand, if it provided value – if the benefits were tangible.

The magnitude of this shift in my life felt worthy of an explanation. There is no anger, no resentment, no bitterness nor any other ill feelings toward the supposed Christian god, toward my parents who introduced me to this god, nor toward any family or friends who continue to worship him. I recognize there is significant consonance between many of the people I know, and the kind of person Christianity attracts and benefits. So, do not interpret these words as trying to persuade anyone from their cherished beliefs. This short note is simply an attempt to explain why I have chosen to walk away from the faith which so many people feel has sustained them in hard times, the hope they have of being reunited with loved ones again in heaven, and the peace they claim "passeth" all understanding.

I have thought more, and even written more, about what I see as the flawed process of Christianity – its problematic *how*. Quite simply, I now see objectivity, or at least the pursuit of it, to be the most effective means by which to learn how the world works, how we as individuals think, and how we should set goals and work to achieve them. I have lost faith in the *how* of Christianity, and subsequently my idea of the Christian god as its result.

Much love to you all.

Your husband, son, brother, uncle, nephew, cousin, and friend,

Luther

Chapter 01

Introduction

Christianity's problematic how can be seen clearly in the Biblical story of Abraham climbing Mount Moriah to sacrifice his son on an altar. If you haven't heard this story or don't remember it, I'll provide the highlights as told in the Book of Exodus.

1) God tells Abraham to sacrifice his son on an altar.
2) Abraham climbs the mountain with his son, builds an altar, and binds his son atop the altar.
3) Abraham raises a knife to kill his son, but God stops him.
4) God provides Abraham with an animal to sacrifice instead.

This story is largely told as God testing Abraham. Some Christians admire the faith of a man who would murder his own son, and others aren't so sure. On the one hand, Abraham was immediately willing to obey a command from God, even though it didn't make sense and seemed out of character for a loving god. But on the other hand, he was going to murder his son. Abraham was handsomely rewarded for passing this oddly barbaric test – he and his descendants, the Jews, became God's chosen people. But almost all the discussion about this story is centered on *what* Abraham believed and *what* he was willing to do. But *how* did Abraham come to learn what God wanted him to do? The Biblical author only mentions that he heard a voice. Just... a voice.

I don't believe anyone should commit violence based on a conversation they had with an invisible being – not the eventual father of Judaism, not modern Christians, and certainly not my daughters. Because hearing that voice was a personal experience for Abraham, neither his wife nor son could corroborate what the voice said, or even if there was a voice at all. Had Abraham been mistaken, there was no way for those who would suffer the most from that mistake to reveal that error to him.

This is a book about hearing voices, reading ancient scriptures, and some of the other personal experiences that Christians interpret to be interactions with the creator of the universe. When we experience things in solitude or arrive at conclusions based on our own experience, wrongness is inevitable. This is not entirely disqualifying for Christianity since all human pursuits of truth and knowledge are vulnerable to our perceptions and biases – "to err is human." But what tools do Christians have to recognize their own wrongness, or to challenge the wrongness of their family, friends, and religious community? How do Christians right a wrong?

Patriarchy has been taught from Christian pulpits for thousands of years by men who claim to have learned God's will through Bible study, prayer, and other personal experiences with him. What recourse have women had throughout the history of Christianity to confront these sexist and discriminatory ideas? What recourse do they have now? Their own Bible study? Their own prayer? Their own personal experiences? Are the experiences of women with God any more credible than the experiences of men with God? These aren't theoretical and unanswerable questions, such as the nature of God or the origin of sin. These questions get to the *how* of Christian living, and impact Christians in their daily lives.

The Abraham story didn't serve as a cautionary tale for my Christianity because I was never going to kill anyone. And although I had Christian family and friends who maintained some strange beliefs, they weren't going to kill anyone either. But what connects so-called moderate versions of Christianity to Abraham and even other deeply problematic variations of Christianity is the problematic *how*, and that's the *how* I used to guide my Christianity and my life for many years.

So many people consider the foundational belief of Christianity to be the saving grace of Jesus Christ. But how does a Christian come to know about Jesus? How do Christians know that he is the literal son of God? How are Christians to know what he is doing now, and what he wants us to be doing? *What* Christians believe about God is predicated on *how* they came to believe it, and because they claim that God has chosen to move throughout the Earth predominantly invisibly, inaudibly, and intangibly, almost all the beliefs and practices of Christianity have been arrived at through personal experiences. To believe in the product of these interactions, a person must first believe that the interactions themselves are credible ways to know things. We should be critical of *how* any knowledge or set of beliefs came to be and is substantiated, but in all my years as a Christian, I never experienced any Christians seriously critiquing the *how* of their beliefs.

David Koresh

I was in high school when David Koresh's Branch Davidian compound in Waco, Texas was surrounded by federal agents. A 51-day standoff ensued and ended abruptly when the compound burned to the ground with Koresh and many others inside. This standoff was particularly relevant in my home because the Branch Davidians were in some way connected to the denomination I was raised in, Seventh-Day Adventism (SDA). Or, maybe David Koresh had attended a few SDA churches. The connection was never clear to me, but the SDA church headquarters felt compelled to write a strong letter condemning Koresh and the Davidians.

More interestingly, though, were the conversations around my own family's dinner table. Aunts, uncles, and cousins all enjoyed a laugh at the expense of Koresh and his followers during the standoff. We didn't laugh at the death of Koresh and his followers, but during the standoff we thought the whole situation was partly hilarious and partly quite sad. Koresh claimed to be the last messiah, as predicted by the Bible, and there were allegations of underage marriage and Koresh taking other men's wives as his own (they always take other men's wives).

We wondered how anyone could believe such ridiculous claims. But it occurred to me that Jesus also claimed to be a messiah who had been predicted by earlier scripture. And further, that Jesus set out to convince a small group that he was sinless, born of a virgin, and would resurrect himself after being killed. I imagined my family, had we lived thousands of years ago, sitting around laughing at Jesus' disciples just as we laughed at Koresh's followers. The wider story of Christianity also now came into focus, but differently. From talking snakes and magical trees to whole-Earth floods and people being raised from the dead, I realized in this moment for the first time how nonsensical these beliefs would seem to an outsider. This was my first realization that I held some outrageous beliefs.

I was not bothered by the actual strangeness of my beliefs, though, since neither a supernatural power nor the natural universe has any obligation to make sense to me. I was bothered because before that moment, I had always considered my beliefs to be very normal. There hadn't been anything outlandish about a creator-god impregnating a young virgin girl with himself so that he could be killed by humans, which would then allow him to save other humans from a hell fire that he would otherwise throw them into because of their disobedience. It was jarring for me to suddenly see my religious beliefs as strange. No less strange, in fact, than ideas such as reincarnation and martyrs being awarded virgins in heaven, which I had always thought to be really, really strange.

I also immediately recognized the role that indoctrination played in my life. I had heard these stories about Jesus and God enough times from enough trusted friends and family members, and everyone around me believed them, so they became normalized. To that point in my life, none of the stories in Bibles sounded the least bit unlikely. But now, recognizing that my beliefs are just as strange as everyone else's, I began to wonder what made my beliefs any more believable than the beliefs of other faiths. And the words of my parents and grandparents were no longer evidence. I wanted some sort of external corroboration.

This is the origin of my pursuit for proof, evidence, and support for my spiritual beliefs. I accepted that extraordinary claims required extraordinary proof, but I had never sought proof for my beliefs because I hadn't seen them as extraordinary. But that had now changed.

The Koresh standoff didn't just plant seeds of doubt about my beliefs – it showed how much I had been shaped by the influences around me. I realized that my beliefs had always felt so natural, not because the stories made sense, but because they were the dominant narrative of my life, repeated by the people I loved and trusted most. But now, I had to confront the fact that just like the followers of David Koresh,

I could be holding on to something simply because it was all I'd ever known. Obviously, that realization didn't lead me to abandon Christianity immediately, but it did spark a journey. A journey that made me curious, made me question, and most importantly, made me open to seeing the world – and myself – differently.

Do you recall the first big question you had about your spiritual beliefs – or other big ideas passed down by your family?

Chapter 02

Subjectivity

Going through puberty began a very complicated and strained relationship between sex and myself, and it didn't end until the day I chose to walk away from Christianity. Before I got married, I was repeatedly told that sex is only for marriage, so I felt guilty before and after every sexual encounter. And because I believed that Jesus died for my sins, my premarital sex was partly responsible for his death on the cross. I eventually worked myself into this convoluted spiritual ideology which held that although I still wanted to keep having sex, I wanted to stop wanting to have sex, which is all God really required of me. The logic may be hard to follow, but this is how I coped with my raging sexual desires and the accompanying guilt... while continuing to have premarital sex.

During my time as a Christian, I met several other believers who were having guilt-free sex before marriage. Some believed the Biblical condemnation of adultery was only for married people, others had their own convoluted spiritual justifications, and a few just flat out ignored the spiritual ramifications of their sexual choices. It was always interesting and then ultimately troubling to meet Christians with widely different views about sex. I met gay Christians who were also struggling to avoid sex, and I heard about gay Christian churches that didn't require or even encourage abstinence.

Aside from sex, there is also widespread disagreement within Christianity regarding gender issues. Some versions of Christianity ordain women to the highest level of priesthood, and others do not. Politically, some Christians cite their faith as justification for supporting Conservative politicians, and others staunchly reject political Conservatism. History tells us that Christianity was used to defend slavery, and as an impetus to abolish it. Even the most apologetic Christian must acknowledge there is a wide range of ideas and beliefs, many in direct conflict with each other, that all sit comfortably under the umbrella of Christianity.

This wasn't a big problem for my family because we love to argue and debate with each other. We can argue for hours about politics, sports, television shows, and which restaurant makes the best French fries. That's why I found it strange when we stopped debating with each other over our spiritual beliefs. Even when we maintained conflicting ideas about Jesus Christ himself, the way he shows love to us, and the way he desires for us to show that love to the world, once a person feels led by God to accept a certain Biblical interpretation, there was little else the others of us could say to convince them otherwise. Our own Biblical interpretations and experiences were just that – our own. So, we accepted that God leads people differently and each has their own Christian journey.

For the Christians outside of my family and friend groups who I had deep disagreements with over political or social issues, at best I accused them of being either confused, selfish, or stubborn. At worst, I decided that those with the most extreme and hurtful beliefs weren't really Christians at all. I couldn't believe that anyone who earnestly prayed, studied the Bible, and had a connection with Jesus Christ would believe and behave in such hurtful ways. But these people didn't see their beliefs as cruel and would likely deny that I was a real Christian based on what I believed and how my Christianity manifested itself. Every person who calls themselves a Christian can claim to be standing on the moral and spiritual high ground simply by attacking the competency or character of other Christians who they claim have problematic beliefs and behaviors.

It became clear to me that all these Christians use the same processes to avoid wrongness that I did, which caused my own feelings of rightness to seem ego based and precarious. Before I ever lost confidence in the totality of Christianity, I lost confidence in the process by which I picked one set of Christian ideals over the others. I had accepted that peace, love, wisdom, joy, and charity were the byproducts of a Christian lifestyle, and I wanted these things for myself and my family. So, I wanted to believe the right Christian things and live the right Christian way. If I had been wrong about something and one of my cousins was right, I wanted to know. But how could one of my cousins package their truth in a way that would be convincing to me? More Bible texts? Logic and reason? What evidence would I accept? What evidence *should* I accept? What evidence can the conservatives present the progressives? What evidence could the abolitionists have presented the slave holders?

These are important questions because our minds are so good at confirmation bias, a process by which we subconsciously prioritize or only see information that confirms what we already believe to be true, and minimize or outright dismiss what contradicts our beliefs. It takes almost no evidence to further entrench a Christian into the brand of Christianity they were raised in or have come to accept. And too often, no amount of evidence, regardless of who presents it or how it is presented, is enough to convince a Christian that even one of their beliefs is problematic. The easily accessible subconscious and conscious processes that people use to stand firm on any one particular belief also make it nearly impossible for them to see *any* of their other beliefs as wrong. This is why a sincere search for truth, whether spiritual or otherwise, must acknowledge and account for our propensity to avoid our own wrongness, and the ease with which we do so.

A belief that is never seen as wrong can never be improved upon by taking new information into account. This is why it's so important for our beliefs to include viable pathways toward being seen as wrong. Religious beliefs, however, are often constructed in ways that preclude them from ever being falsified – there is no outcome, experiment, or circumstance that could disprove the principle claims of almost every faith-based belief system. Unfalsifiable beliefs are so dangerous because we have such imaginative minds, as evidenced by the litany of past and present world religions, as well as the past scientific theories that have been debunked. The differences between the denominations of Christianity, such as Baptist, Pentecostal, Catholic, and Lutheran are all protected by unfalsifiability. The differences between Christianity, Hinduism, and the Church of Scientology are all protected by unfalsifiability. Suicide cults and unscrupulous miracle healers thrive on unfalsifiable claims.

Throughout history, humanity has attributed successful crop growth, womb health, and even the movement of the stars in the night sky to the works of one god or another. Even now, when someone narrowly avoids a car accident or is suddenly cured of an ailment, many would ascribe those outcomes to the purposeful intervention of the Christian god. While some believe that hurricanes form due to rapidly rising warm air from the ocean surface, others believe the devil precipitates these conditions to cause human suffering, and yet others believe that God sends hurricanes to punish particularly wicked cities. The latter two explanations are protected by unfalsifiability and will never be disproven. Falsifiability opens for us the necessary pathways toward wrongness, which precedes any correction toward an improved understanding of ourselves and the universe we live in. When wrongness is hard to come by, our belief systems run wildly unchecked to the furthest domains of human imagination or suffer the equally perilous fate of remaining stagnant and reliant on old schools of thought.

I was trained as a scientist, and laboratory research affords scientists the opportunity to be wrong all the time. I've run many experiments and interpret data all by myself in the laboratory, only to make unexplainable mistakes that were caught by other colleagues reviewing the work. My research groups have submitted our findings for publication, and had other scientists notice things in our data that we hadn't. It became clear to me that the biases and assumptions we brought into the lab impacted the way we saw and interpreted results, and it was humbling to experience my own intuition, and even my vision, be misled by what I expected to see or thought I knew. This forced me to face the limitations of my perspective, and to accept what many other scientists know to be true – the human is the most flawed instrument in any scientific experiment.

I don't know if Christianity affords believers those same opportunities for blatant wrongness, which can lead to humility toward our perspectives and intuitions. Are all scientists humble? No, not even close. But my experience with science is what humbled me, and I don't recall many moments in my Christian journey that forced me to confront my own wrongness. I was rarely challenged in ways that forced me to concede that any of my strongly held beliefs were incorrect, or that my perspective was inherently limited. Science, reason, and logic have been the better tools to help me see the limitations of human perspective and observation.

Scientists are not better people than Christians, and they are no less prone to mistakes or character flaws. Scientists also want to avoid being corrected or seen as wrong, and both consciously and subconsciously work to prevent this from happening. Every historical breakdown in the scientific process has resulted from the acceptance of data and analysis from limited perspectives. This happens when individuals or homogeneous groups regard themselves as super observers who can put aside their biases, desires, and preconceived notions to inerrantly analyze data and draw conclusions. The "science" that emerges from these scenarios is almost always embarrassingly overturned when the conclusions are subjected to verification by more diverse observers.

We all must see our intuitions as biased, our perspectives as limited, and our analyses as susceptible to influences that may even be unknown to us. I am ever aware of the potentially unbounded distortion of my subjective lenses, so the validation of my most consequential beliefs and ideas now only occurs through the recruitment and acceptance of diverse observers and perspectives. This is the pursuit of objectivity, which is needed to check and balance rampant subjectivity.

A public experience is one in which the things I see, hear, or feel would also be seen, heard, or felt by another person, regardless of their age, gender, socioeconomic status, political affiliation, religious beliefs, ethnic background, or association with me. On the other hand, personal experiences are unique to an individual or shared by very small groups that are like minded in some way, so they cannot be verified or corroborated. Because our subjective biases color the way we interpret *all* our experiences, true objectivity is practically impossible. We are not limited to the dichotomy of having fully subjective or fully objective beliefs. We can work to counteract some of the errors attributable to our subjective biases and limited perspective. The goal is not objectivity, but instead less subjective bias.

Subjectivity has its merits and provides for beautiful expressions and experiences throughout our lives. It is not my intention to disparage subjectivity, but it can be a problematic tool in the search for universal truth and what is real. Our past personal experiences, expectations, and a host of other individual attributes can drastically alter our perception of reality. Public experiences allow for consensus building from diverse observers with differing biases and perspectives, revealing a less altered reality. What do Christians and Muslims both see? What do the rich and poor both hear? What do the old and young both feel? If the Christians, Muslims, rich, poor, old, and young all share an experience, this is more objective than something experienced by an individual in solitude. For the task at hand – finding out how the world works and how we should exist in it – less subjective bias is better than more subjective bias; more objectivity is better than less objectivity.

Granted, we don't have the luxury to pursue objectivity in most of our daily activities. We are often wholly dependent on our subjective interpretation of events and circumstances, as we would experience paralysis by analysis if we second-guessed or sought additional perspectives on everything we saw, felt, and heard throughout the day. As a result of this, we've necessarily built up a fair bit of confidence in our ability to experience the world as it is. But this confidence becomes problematic when the opportunity to confirm our perspectives and ideas through more objective channels is available, and we resist doing so because we don't think we need to. This kind of ego is the breeding ground for so many harmful yet eradicable ideas such as racism, sexism, and homophobia. Not coincidentally, Christianity has been one of the most prolific perpetrators of these three specific ideas, and is still struggling to extricate itself from their harmful premises. Constructing a world view dominated by our own perspectives, and the experiences of those who are like us in significant ways, is perilous and irresponsible, at best.

The larger problem with subjectivity is its tenuous relationship with wrongness, and how difficult it can be to convince someone that what they saw, heard, or felt isn't exactly how things happened. Belief systems built on subjectivity are effectively unfalsifiable, and this is Christianity.

As a child, I learned about the Biblical parable of the foolish man who built his house on the sand, and the wise man who built his house on the rock. Both houses stood tall as long as the sun shone, but when the winds, rain, and floods came, the house built on rock remained and the house built on sand fell. Hearing and obeying the words of Jesus Christ were likened unto building one's house on a solid rock foundation. And indeed, Christianity does often look solidly constructed and is even largely functional. But Christianity is built on the deeply flawed foundation of rampant subjectivity.

As a Christian, I brought my experiences, biases, assumptions, desires, and fears to my understanding of Jesus Christ, and then tuned my version of Christianity to those ideas. As my life changed and my experiences grew, my views about Jesus also changed. This vulnerability to human subjectivity explains why Christianity can be so beautiful at times, and also very ugly. It explains why there are so many different denominations of believers who all embrace the same Bible, why different versions of the Bible conflict with each other, why groups of Christians promote certain translations and disparage others, why well-meaning Christians hurt the people they love, and why some believers have abundant peace and others have crippling guilt.

Just as the house built on sand looked good when the sun was shining, Christianity's foundation looks solid when Christians attribute their generous behaviors and peace of mind to their faith in Jesus Christ. When Christians suddenly feel impressed to help a stranger, or through prayer and Bible study feel convicted to build hospitals and schools, Christianity's foundation appears solid as a rock.

I used to think that faith and Christianity were most critically challenged during personal crises such as unexpected tragedies or financial hardships, but even the most absurd forms of Christianity survive these kinds of tests. I've since recognized that the winds, rain, and flood waters that most consistently and alarmingly expose the flawed foundation of Christianity are the moments when professed believers have harmful ideas and then attribute those ideas to the Christian god. The processes of Christianity reveal themselves to be flawed when well-meaning Christians mistake the natural for the supernatural – when people wrongly believe their own desires are God's desires, and their own morality is God's morality.

The most extreme and harmful versions of Christianity are identical in process to the more peaceful and charitable versions – individuals end prayers, close their Bibles, and drive away from church believing they have heard the voice of God and feel obligated to obey, even if the commands do not make sense. I am not criticizing *what* any Christian believes as much as I take issue with the process by which they come to those beliefs, how dependent those beliefs are on subjective experiences, and their resulting unfalsifiability.

Science also continues to be directly responsible for varying levels of malfeasance, but the most harmful scientific outcomes are not born out of the same processes used to achieve good science. And scientific methods have changed through the years as we've learned more about biases, perspectives, and how subjectivity impacts our findings – double blind research studies didn't exist 100 years ago. On the other hand, Christians interact with their god now the same way they did 2,000 years ago.

I grew up in a church that previously demonized the wearing of jewelry, and many women were deeply hurt and had their characters attacked due to the church's stance. A few holdouts still cling to the idea that jewelry is immodest, but they have become the silent minority. This small group has never been forced to confront their wrongness, but I don't recall any discussions among those who now accept jewelry about how that wrongness initially became a widely accepted truth, and how it remained that way for decades. Were Bible texts misunderstood? Was the urging of the holy spirit misinterpreted? Was church leadership guided by something other than God?

These are the questions that wrongness forces us to confront and addressing them openly and honestly can prevent similar mistakes from being repeated. But this didn't happen. It didn't happen 20 years ago with jewelry, and it didn't happen 50 years ago when this same church eventually decided that it should no longer bar its ministers from presiding over interracial marriages. And now they are grappling over their current rule prohibiting women from being fully credentialed members of the clergy. So, expectedly, both sides first hurl Bible verses and then insults, both sides have prayed, and both sides feel convicted of God's will. And regardless of what the church decides to do, either by vote or by decree, there will be no great reckoning about who was wrong and why. No one will approach their beliefs in the future with greater humility because of a more accurate understanding of their subjective fallibilities. This has unfortunately been the repeated cycle throughout the long history of Christianity, and there is no institutional knowledge or improvement to its processes to show for it.

Christianity is wholly dependent on human subjectivity, and there has been no substantive acknowledgment of the problems that result because of this, and hence no attempts to overcome them. This is Christianity's problematic *how*, its sinking sand, and it is dangerous, pervasive, and undeniable.

Brooches

(To the best of my knowledge, brooch and its plural, brooches, are the only English words where a 'double o' makes a **long o** sound, like in go and bro. So, even though it doesn't look like it should, brooch rhymes with coach, and brooches rhymes with coaches. No, I cannot answer any more questions about this pronunciation.)

The Seventh-Day Adventist (SDA) Church used to be strongly against wearing jewelry – even wedding bands were discouraged. At my parents' wedding, my father gave my mother a watch instead of a ring. And at my wedding 40 years later, the minister didn't allow rings to be exchanged during the service, so we quickly slipped them onto our fingers in the limousine on the way to the reception.

When I was a teenager, women who wore rings, earrings, and necklaces were associated with Jezebel, a spiritual "harlot" in the Bible. The church used an interpretation of scripture to support their stance, and since God wrote the Bible, wearing jewelry was considered to be an act of protest and defiance to God himself.

It was okay, however, to wear brooches to church. These might be out of style now, but they were basically bejeweled lapel pins, and all the adult SDA women I knew wore them proudly because they weren't considered to be jewelry. Yes, you read that correctly, be-JEWEL-ed lapel pins weren't considered to be JEWEL-ry. The same women who discouraged others from wearing rings and earrings were the ones who routinely wore brooches. But my problem wasn't that the church was preaching an inconsistent view. That certainly isn't ideal or commendable, but that's not what makes the acceptance of brooches so memorable and ultimately play such an important role in my decision to leave Christianity. The problem was that I didn't see this inconsistency until I was in college. And even then, it took someone else to point it out.

All my life, I had been staring at jewelry on the lapels of almost every woman in the church, but I wasn't calling it jewelry because I simply didn't see it as jewelry. I had been conditioned to see brooches as something else, but they are definitely jewelry. This was a blind spot, and it ultimately changed the way I viewed all my beliefs. What else wasn't I seeing? What other obvious blind spots were lurking amongst my most strongly held beliefs?

This realization didn't just change how I saw jewelry – it obviously changed how I saw myself. Missing something so obvious for so long made me more aware of potential blind

24

spots, even in the things I believed most deeply – the things I accepted as part of my faith. I began to understand that faith is likely flawed because we are flawed. So, I could no longer trust faith alone as a way of understanding the world. I needed something more reliable, something that accounted for those blind spots, and I began valuing and pursuing objectivity. This still wasn't the end of my spiritual journey, but it was a shift – one that allowed me to see both myself and the world more clearly.

Have you confronted any major blind spots from your upbringing – spiritual or otherwise?

Chapter 03

Faith

I have been asked if there is anything that could cause me to rethink my disbelief in the Christian god and his love for humanity. The answer is a resounding yes, and I can list a hundred such things quite easily. They all revolve around the idea of objective verifiability, but this is not how the Christian god seems to operate. Christians must experience their god by faith.

Faith lacks a singular definition and is not limited to religious contexts. It can refer to complete trust or confidence in something, such as the expectation that gravity will bring a person back down after jumping on a trampoline. Faith can also refer to a belief maintained despite contrary, limited, or debatable evidence. This aligns with the Biblical instruction to "walk by faith, not by sight." So, in this discussion, faith will specifically refer to beliefs that rely on insufficient evidence to convince most reasonable people.

By contrast, when evidence is so compelling that nearly everyone, regardless of cultural background, education, or worldview, accepts it as true, belief in that idea can be considered something other than faith. For example, belief in gravity is not considered faith here because its behavior is so widely predictable and accepted.

Alternatively, logic, reason, and evidence-based practices are also available to help us learn how the world works, how our minds and bodies work, where we came from, and what we might become. Christians don't deny these other tools, and often use them to construct their own versions of Christianity, just as I still exercise faith in people and ideas. My discord with Christianity centers around the prioritization of ideas and information gathered through faith and spiritual discernment above what is generated through evidence-seeking methods and what has been subjected to reason and logical analysis. Christianity requires faith to sit atop the hierarchy of all tools available for belief building, so that when conflict arises between what these methods conclude, spiritual discernment will always overrule scientific evidence and logical analysis.

For this reason, scientific challenges, historical discrepancies, and logical fallacies will almost never invalidate faith because Christians have not given these tools the agency to do so. This is not to say that what Christians believe is illogical; that is a debate to be had by people much smarter than me. But if it were shown that Christianity at its core is illogical, Christians would not en masse abandon their belief in it.

In its elevated position, faith can overcome any obstacle put forward by these other tools, but by being so resistant to evidence and by not being confined by reason, faith can also overcome the blatant contradictions and nonsensical beliefs associated with suicidal cults and for-profit preachers. Incontestable faith essentially asks its practitioners to ignore what is evident, or to take as evidence what is unverifiable by others, leaving faith seekers dangerously vulnerable. Absolute faith is the currency that can keep any false religions or cults in business, but many believers only see this vulnerability as problematic for other people's religious convictions, not their own.

Some Christians claim there *is* overwhelming evidence to support the existence of God, authority of the Bible, divinity of Jesus, and intelligent design of the universe. But because there are more non-Christians than Christians in the world, spiritual discernment has clearly not led to the kind of evidence that can convince *any* reasonable person of Christ's divinity. So, by the above definition, faith is at work. Biblical authors knew that no evidence existed for Christ's birth to a virgin, his resurrection, or heavenly home, so they relied upon and promoted faith, with one author going so far as to write that faith itself is evidence. Elsewhere, Bibles suggest that faith is required to please God. Faith is a constant theme throughout the New Testament, suggesting that those who lived just decades after the death and resurrection of their savior relied heavily on faith. And in the two thousand years since the Bible was written, no information has been gained to make faith less necessary today. Faith is required of all Christians.

Even if the existence of a supernatural being could be verified without faith, and even if this being was objectively proven to have created life on Earth, faith would still be required to believe his character to be perfect, his human birth to a virgin, his resurrection, ascension, and ultimate reward of heaven. Christianity has taken the common feeling of something greater than humanity existing in the universe and turned it into a very detailed story about good and evil beings, and the creator of the universe walking alongside men, and then being murdered for the benefit of his believers. Some measure of faith is required to believe in this story, and then to depend upon the protagonist for peace of mind and life purpose.

If a person starts with the belief in the Christian god, and finding no proof of this god is told that faith itself can be proof, not only will they value faith, but they will value it above reason, logic, science, and history since these tools had been incapable of confirming God's existence. The evidence-based methods have so far been unable to corroborate the god that Christians so clearly see through the lens of faith, so these other methods are seen as not entirely competent. Christians view the awareness of Christ as the most important thing that can be known or discovered, and because faith alone provides this awareness, it is given priority status atop all the other tools available for discovering truth and forming beliefs. Because of this status, not only will faith be used to support beliefs that lack scientific or historical proof, but it will also be used to ignore logical fallacies and to disparage challenges from all other evidence-seeking approaches. This is how faith establishes its credibility, by being the only method that can confirm the Christian's belief in a loving man-god who created the universe. Belief in the Christian god is what motivates the elevated view of faith in a person's life, and in turn that faith is what validates their belief in God.

These two premises, the existence of God and the elevated role of faith, form a circular belief system, meaning that neither can be accepted without first believing the other. The existence of God would first need to be accepted to hold faith in such high regard, but faith must first be held in high regard to believe in the Christian God.

The value of childhood indoctrination is clear when it's understood how circular arguments can be used to support each other. Before I learned about reason, evidence, and facts, I was told several million times that the Christian god is real. This belief then established the elevated value of faith when I became an adult, and for many years that faith was used to substantiate my belief in Jesus Christ. When I was a Christian, I saw contradictions and holes in the narrative, but those issues were *covered* by faith. I simply never asked what authority faith had to overcome these challenges, and how faith earned this authority.

In practice, faith-based tools and evidence-generating pursuits are both prone to failure. Even if each tool itself is perfect, the errancy of human observers diminishes its capabilities and should lower our confidence in its output. On this point, human errancy, is where my beliefs diverge from how Christians must view themselves, and this underscores everything I've written here. Knowing that human perception is so easily manipulated and can be influenced by our desires, fears, and biases, some way of verifying information is warranted. And extraordinary claims warrant extraordinary proof.

Proof is needed because peer pressure, gullibility, wishful thinking, tradition, thoughtlessness, and a host of other problematic motivators can be mistaken for evidence and can masquerade as faith. Sending money to the television evangelist is not always an act of faith and can instead be the result of gullibility. Choosing to ignore information that contradicts a firmly held belief can be trumpeted as faith but may really be a resistance to thinking deeply about or adding layers of nuance to a problem previously thought to have a straightforward solution.

Wishful thinking occurs when a person forms beliefs largely based on what they *want* to be true. Wanting a friend or family member to be cured of an illness motivates the belief that God *will* perform a miracle. This false reality is exacerbated when the believer operates upon that belief as if it were faith, or relates it to others as faith. Once a person decides or declares they are acting in faith, even if the true sources of their actions are gullibility and wishful thinking, it becomes completely acceptable for them to act irrationally and to ignore family members, friends, doctors, lawyers, scientists, historians, and their own priest or pastor. Invoking the term "faith" not only allows a believer to press forward in opposition to evidence, but often also garners the admiration and support of other believers.

Wishful thinking and other subjective issues can also corrupt evidence-based practices. The scientific process can be ill-applied, and historical sources can be erroneously favored over others, all to support a desired conclusion. Financial incentives, egotism, and even bigotry have always plagued and still taint evidence-based practices, and this has rightfully caused skepticism toward new scientific or historical findings with any social relevance. But whereas subjectivity is considered to plague the pursuit of evidence, it is the hallmark of the Christian experience through spiritual discernment.

Subjectivity can impact findings even from well-meaning individuals with neither explicit nor implicit biases. The potential for human error cannot be overstated and is not limited to individuals since whole groups routinely fall prey to charismatic preaching and wishful thinking. People make mistakes. As much as I love and respect my grandparents, I see them as innately human in their ability to believe things that are not true. I see my parents this way and the rest of my family and friends this way. I see all the world's top scientists and historians this way, as well as the Biblical authors, the Buddha, and David Koresh. Most importantly, however, I see myself this way. So, before I can accept any statement as truth, I must insist on some method of verification or truth testing to counteract human errancy.

I did not find reliable methods for truth testing within Christianity, which makes extraordinary claims about the origins of the universe and the afterlife. Claims about the world should be refutable by the world, and the primary claim of Christianity is that a loving god exists, but there is no series of events, no scientific experiment, nor circumstance that believers can find themselves in, that can refute that claim. There are no checks and balances to rampant speculation posed in the form of an irrefutable claim. Christians are free to maintain any imaginable idea of God, our history, and even the future of mankind, all without being accountable to the natural universe. There are currently thousands of these faith-based practices that all rely heavily on irrefutable claims, which makes Christianity unremarkable in this regard.

Christians must wait until the afterlife to have their faith justified. While living here on Earth though, Christians must see faith as the substitute for proof, the rebuttal to evidence, and the antidote to doubt. Since I no longer find faith more credible or convincing than testable evidence and the pursuit of objectivity, I derive no comfort in irrefutable claims, and I find no solid evidence for Christ.

If the Christian god is as real and all-knowing as believers claim him to be, then he is not surprised that myself and others like me have no confidence in the subjective process of Christianity. If he really chose the processes of prayer, Bible study, and miracles as the pathways to know and fall in love with him, then my disbelief, however unintended it may have been, was well expected. I am always open to new information and new evidence, but I do not expect the Christian god to become evident in my lifetime. I am willing to accept that there is no pathway to truth for me in Christianity since my standard for evidence is different than the Christian standard, so my faith cannot be redeemed through ancient books, sermons, vague prophecies, and medical recoveries.

I know many Christians who apply a highly critical standard to facts, evidence, and the conclusions drawn from such, for matters outside of their spiritual life, but then choose not to apply that same level of scrutiny to their religious beliefs. Some Christians even claim that matters of spirituality are beyond the reach of human reason and logic, but I can no longer accept this. I listen to religious testimonies with the same ears that I hear scientific lectures, and reaching unsupported conclusions or ignoring the impact of personal bias is problematic in both arenas. There is a place for faith in my life, but I have not given it jurisdiction to overrule challenges from other more objective tools.

I do not understand why a god who is real and all powerful would relegate himself to the same existence as the thousands of other false gods who have occupied only the minds of their believers, and who are only interacted with through faith and subjective experiences. I do not understand why a real god would allow himself to be misrepresented by those who seek to misuse his name, and misunderstood by those who genuinely want to know him. If I can think of 100 ways that an all-knowing god can become evident and reveal to humanity his true character and desires, surely, he could think of many more.

I do not spend much time wondering why any god hasn't or wouldn't make his existence known in more objectively verifiable ways. I recognize that if an all-knowing god exists, his motivations would be well beyond my, or any other human's, understanding. Even my desire for a more evident existence could be considered presumptuous. But if a higher power asks me to participate in some sort of cosmic exercise, either through belief or some action, and there are many such gods to choose from, it does become my prerogative to seek clarity. If a god asks me to choose him above all others, and he instilled in me the ability to use reason and logic, then my application of these tools should be welcomed.

Homosexuality

In graduate school, I learned about gay Christian churches being started in California. I had read that "Homosexuality is an abomination" in Leviticus and by that time had heard dozens of sermons that detailed a hard line, Bible-based admonition against homosexuality. But I knew that gay Christians were not stupid, and surely, they had also read the Levitical text, so I was curious to read about how they "got around" these things. I went online and found a brief pamphlet outlining every Biblical mention of Homosexuality, and an alternate more gay-friendly way to interpret the texts.

For instance, these gay Christians believed that God made Adam and Eve (not Adam and Steve) because he needed procreation, but that no longer is a priority today. They believe the Levitical text was indeed a command from God, but only for the Children of Israel, who also needed to rapidly increase their numbers. In the New Testament, Paul says that homosexuality is unnatural, but this was seen as a statement of ignorance from Paul, not God. They reasoned that Paul wrote what he believed to be true, but simply wasn't aware of all the natural instances of homosexuality in the animal kingdom.

I was not immediately convinced by these alternative interpretations of scripture which suggested that a person could be unrepentantly homosexual *and* Christian, although I would eventually come to accept this belief. But a more deeply rooted seed had been planted after reading these interpretations: the methods used to interpret scripture in support of homosexual Christian churches were not any different than the methods my denomination had used to support so many of its beliefs. The interpretations go something like this: "In this text, God is speaking to all people for all time, but in this text, he is only speaking to the immediate audience. In this text, God is speaking, and in this other text, Paul is speaking from his own perspective."

I did not see any clues in the Bible to help decipher who was *really* speaking, and who was the intended audience. On the topic of homosexuality, no outrageous logical leaps were required to move forward with a gay Christian church, at least no more outrageous than what was needed to support other beliefs I held. I felt as though two reasonable minds could disagree. Non footnoted footnote: there is more discussion of this in the chapter about Bibles.

Many Christians are happy to accept that two people may feel inspired by God to believe two different things about homosexuality, but this was deeply problematic to me. I imagined two gay people getting up from their personal Bible study, one feeling their sexual activity is okay and the other feeling that their behavior is hated by God, and they spend the rest of their life trying not to act on those urges. Others languish in uncertainty throughout their whole life, finding it difficult to commit to either lifestyle because of this uncertainty. It's one thing to know what is right, and to choose wrong. It's another to believe you are doing right but actually doing wrong. At the other end of this, how many parents thought they were being good Christians by turning their backs on their own children who came out the closet? It's not okay for well-intentioned people to have such varying views about something so impactful to their lives and well beings, and it seems to me that a personal God could easily make this clear.

Maybe this ambiguity is not okay with God either. Maybe it pains him to see people struggle to know what is right, and maybe he has reasons for not clarifying his views. But I had been taught that Bibles were to help us arbitrate these types of issues. I thought Bibles were supposed to clarify God's will, what we believe and why, but on this issue it fails. Perhaps I had unrealistic expectations of Bibles, but now my perception had certainly changed, and those expectations went through the floor. Bibles seemed powerless as an arbitrator at a time when so many issues need clarity, and I was no longer sure where that clarity could come from. My beliefs now felt rudderless, only backed up by how true a particular interpretation of scripture felt to myself and my spiritual community. There was no way to settle disagreements between earnest, truth-seeking Christians, and this was problematic.

But how had disagreements between Christians ever been settled? The disciples apparently cast straws to determine God's selection for the man who would replace Judas as a disciple. In 325 CE, whether Jesus was the literal son of God was taken to a vote among religious scholars. The Seventh-Day Adventist Church recently voted on the issue of women's ordination, and they voted against it – *not* to ordain women. Is voting how God's will is determined, because this doesn't seem okay to me. And how does the need for drawing straws and voting in the corporate church structure translate to my own personal search for truth? This is the role I thought Bibles played, but no more, and I desired a more reliable rudder.

This realization marked another turning point in my faith journey. For the first time, I began to see the Bible not as a clear and unwavering guide, but as a text that left too many important questions unresolved. It bothered me that something as fundamental as human identity and love could be interpreted so many different ways by people earnestly seeking the same god. I had been told that God's word was meant to provide clarity and direction, but it left too many people in doubt or despair. I could no longer rely on scripture or personal interpretation to find truth.

Is flexibility in interpretation a strength or a weakness in religious belief? Does it allow for personal growth and adaptability, or does it create confusion and make truth harder to find?

Chapter 04

An Idea

If Jesus Christ could be distilled down to a select set of principles he is said to have promoted, such as loving thy neighbor and taking care of the poor, many Buddhists and Jains would also be followers of Christ. Christians are also not entitled to merely believe in something out there greater than humanity, such as a life force or energy that works in and through everything. A follower of Christ must believe there is one higher power, and he became a man named Jesus who walked the earth, was killed, raised from the dead, and then returned to heaven, and that this process absolved humanity from the deadly consequences of disobeying him. A follower of Christ must also believe Jesus was present at creation and will live eternally, has perfect character, is all powerful and all knowing. Christians must believe that Jesus is God in such a way that to follow Jesus is to follow God, and to learn about God is to learn about Jesus.

I refer to Jesus Christ, God the Father, and the Holy Spirit collectively here as the Christian god, and the process of following this god – of being Christian – necessarily must begin with an understanding of who this god is. If the three are truly one entity, then isolating and putting forward only the life and teachings of Jesus Christ as the tenants of Christianity ignores the larger picture of who he is and sets aside valuable insight toward understanding his character.

A decision to become Christian is not solely based on an awareness that Jesus and his heavenly father exists, but further depends on a determination that this being has perfect character and is worthy to be praised. As humans, we judge each other's character when deciding who to hire, vote for, or befriend, although it's impossible to see the intent of people's actions. We must make assumptions about their motives based on our prior experiences with them, or with others who have acted similarly. Our own biases and preconceived notions about people also play a significant role in these character judgments. And from these assumptions, we decide if a person is trustworthy and dependable, conniving and unscrupulous, or somewhere in between. Despite the shortcomings in this process, these types of subjective judgments form the basis of human relationships. And while some people seem to be better judges of character than others, no one is above being mistaken or intentionally misled.

Judging the character of an invisible god is then even more challenging because not only are the intents of his actions obscured, but so are the actions themselves. No person can verifiably say what the Christian god is doing or has done, so his actions are assumed based on an individual's understanding about what God *would* do, or what they believe he has done in the past, even though these past actions were probably also assumed. What people will believe God has done is a function of their feelings toward him and their judgment of his character. And in circular fashion, people's feelings about God are then influenced by what they have concluded to be his actions. This feedback loop is not informed by any actual observation of God's actions and can lead to conflicting claims about what he has done. No Christian can provide objective evidence to dispute what another Christian claims God is doing. And if two Christians claim that God is doing drastically different things, it is natural for them to disagree about the kinds of things God would do, and even who he is. By not being directly observable, this Christian god has effectively ceded his identity and character to the whims of human opinions, feelings and imaginings.

Although I speak of the Christian god in this way, I do not mean to imply that he is an actual being. I do not believe he exists in any tangible or visible form, but he certainly exists in the minds of his believers. Although Christians look forward to being able to touch him and see him, and they read old stories about those who claimed to experience him in a tangible form, faith would be required of me to experience this Christian god in my lifetime. I am happy to use the definition of faith put forth in Bibles as the substance of things hoped for and the evidence of things not seen. The Christian god is now only accessible through thought, an internal process, rather than through the senses by which we perceive external stimuli. So, just like every other god from every other religion both past and present, the Christian god cannot be touched, heard, or seen except through the lens of faith. He exists within his believers, in their minds as an idea, in as many different variations as there are people who believe in him. Each person has their own idea of who and what he is, because God can be different things to different people. Predictably, then, these ideas conflict with each other and lead to confusion and uncertainty. After thousands of years, preachers and authors still work to clarify this idea of the Christian god in believers.

My grandparents handed their idea of the Christian god to my parents as children, who then shaped and crafted this idea based on their own individual life experiences. When I was a child, my parents told me stories, introduced me to the Bible, prayed with me, and handed their ideas of the Christian god to me, which I gladly accepted because that's what children do. I then began shaping and crafting this idea based upon my own perspective and experiences, and it wasn't long into my adulthood that my idea of God became noticeably different than the ideas my grandparents once held. In other Christian homes, children learned variant ideas about the Christian god from their parents. And others are handed an idea of God from preachers and books, and each person molds that idea based on the disparate lives they lead. Because of this process, and the lack of any verifiable details about what God is doing and why, who each person believes the Christian god to be is primarily the confluence of evolved ideas that have been shaped by our own perspective and biases, and those of our parents, friends, preachers, and teachers.

Whereas I used to believe that subjective issues and disagreements floated on the surface of a deep body of objective knowledge and understanding of the Christian god, I now recognize that literally everything people claim to know about this god is unsubstantiable. I had assumed that details about the life of Christ were corroborated by numerous historical artifacts and documents outside of the Bible. I had assumed it would take a fool to ignore the mountain of evidence that must exist about a man who made the blind to see and fed 5,000 from five loaves and two fish. But when I searched for these other sources, I was underwhelmed. Outside of the Bible, scarcely little is said about the man named Jesus, and even the veracity of these accounts is not a foregone conclusion. My goal here is not to cast aspersions, but to explain that evidence-based methods are not conclusive regarding the ministry of a middle eastern man named Jesus who claimed to be the one true God.

The stories about Jesus and the idea of the Christian god are old, however, and have reached every nation, and have been accepted by almost all my family and many of my friends. I previously mistook these facts about the *idea* of God as validation of God himself. But not all old and widely accepted ideas are founded on truth, and the endurance of an idea is not evidence of its validity. Even the ability of an idea to impart hope, strengthen relationships, or change a person's behavior provides no confirmation of its underlying truthfulness. The power of an idea is derived from each believer's certainty of its truth, not its factual accuracy.

I now recognize that disagreements within the body of believers are not the fault of any misguided person or group but are inherent to the process itself. As long as the Christian god remains intangible, invisible, and inaudible, he will remain an idea, and his believers are left to nurture this idea without objective guidance. Unscrupulous individuals are also free to mold this idea of him however they desire with no fear of being contradicted by the observable world, as long as they avoid predicting specific events at specific times. Ideas that have been handed down through several generations, having been steered by subjectivity without the checks and balances of objective experiences and verifiable evidence will drift and diverge. There should be no surprise, then, that disagreements and confusion have arisen not only between major Christian denominations such as Pentecostal and

Baptist, but also between individual churches within these denominations, between members in the pews, husbands and wives, siblings, parents and their children.

As a child, I was taught about Jesus Christ through facts not derived from objectivity, along with a process of Bible study and prayer that is ruled by subjectivity. I had formed my idea of God through a process perilously at the mercy of my own personal biases and my own feelings. I can no longer count on this process to reliably reveal truth or an explanation of what is real, and I have no desire to harbor an idea that has no value in my life.

God ideas have diverged, and who I wanted God to be was ultimately no more defensible than the Christian gods that lived or currently live in the minds of the slaveholders, abolitionists, witch burners, hospital builders, or pacifists. The process on which Christianity is built gives subjectivity precedence over objectivity, so it is no surprise that biases, traditions, personalities, and vivid imaginings command the highest authority when learning about Jesus Christ. This is Christianity. This is how truth is manifest in Christianity, and this is how the Christian god is experienced and conveyed to new generations of believers.

Give Me the Peace

My wife and I had been in the delivery room most of the night when the doctor came in and said a Cesarean section surgery would be necessary. This was not welcome news, but my immediate goal was to put on a good face for my wife. You know, the "Everything is going to be okay" face. They ushered her out of the room, left me some surgical scrubs, and said they'd be back for me in a few minutes.

I tried to remain calm, but to no avail. My anxiety went immediately through the roof as my mind filled with thoughts of losing my wife or the baby. I began to repeatedly pray, "I need the peace. Jesus, give me the peace. I need the peace. Jesus, give me the peace" – over and over again.

I was at a point in my relationship with God that I no longer asked him for physical things or specific outcomes. One of my cousins who wasn't religious at the time had recently suggested to me that the people who are praying don't have the same things the people who are not praying don't have, and the people who are not praying have the same things the people who are praying have. To put this simply, in a room full of people, with some praying and some not, there's no perceptible difference between what the two groups have.

And it isn't just cars, jobs, and a husband or wife, but also health, divorce, rape, etc. None of these things are exclusive or inclusive to any religious group, so this was his argument against praying for things, and his logic resonated with me. Although Christians ask and ask, no one knows when the Christian god will and when he won't answer yes to requests for tangible blessings. Asking for *things* always felt like a crap shoot, but I believed God can always grant us peace of mind. So, this is what I prayed for, "Jesus, give me the peace. Jesus, give me the peace." But nothing happened. I was still anxious.

It then occurred to me that my faithlessness was responsible for this anxiety. Either I believed God was in control, or I didn't. Either I believed God loved my wife and I, or I didn't. I simply needed to exercise my faith in God. I needed to remember God is in control. And just like that... I felt a blanket of calmness come over me that warmed my entire body. I now stood in the room with complete comfort and in perfect peace. Whatever was about to happen, I knew God was in control and his will would be done. The nurses knocked on the door and escorted me toward the operating room.

As I walked down the hallway in complete peace, a troubling thought pierced through my mind. If I hadn't prayed to God, or believed in Jesus, but instead had prayed to a false god... wouldn't I still have gained peace? If I had prayed to the ancient African fertility goddess Ashanti and truly believed that she would take care of my wife, I could have experienced a similarly peaceful mindset. I realized that while I had been standing in that room waiting, nothing about my circumstances changed. I hadn't been given any updates, and my wife's surgery hadn't started. In those moments, the god I prayed to hadn't really flexed any real power yet. At most, he had just listened, and it seemed to me that anyone can think any god is listening, and that feeling of being heard, that idea of being valuable to something very powerful, creates peace.

The power had actually been flexed by my own mind. The power to believe, and gain peace, was my own. In that moment, I was too distracted by the impending birth to give more thought to this, but when I came back to it months later, I realized our mind's ability to have faith is far more consequential than the object of that faith. I could believe in all sorts of foolishness, and many people do, but if I truly believed it, I could have peace of mind. The power to experience peace of mind rests within us.

This realization was both liberating and unsettling. On the one hand, I was comforted by the idea that peace wasn't something I had to wait for or request from an external source. It was within me all along, and I had the power to access it whenever I needed. But on the other hand, this shifted my relationship with the Christian faith. I had always thought of prayer as a direct line to something greater, something outside myself. Now, I realized it was more about tapping into my own inner strength and belief.

This shift didn't make the Christian faith bad or wrong – it just no longer held the unique power in my life I once believed it did. Peace of mind was literally the last thing I sought the Christian god for. So now, if I can get peace of mind from any belief system, the Christian god became even further inessential. I simply didn't see the value in prayer anymore, or having faith in the Christian god.

What things did you once believe were powerful, useful, or valuable but now recognize as ordinary?

Chapter 05

Discernment

Christianity is the belief in and decision to follow Jesus Christ. But before anyone can follow Jesus, they must know something about him or hear something from him. And since he chooses not to be directly seen or heard, God must *reveal* himself or his will through revelations. Bibles couldn't have been written without God revealing stories, prophecies, and visions to dozens of authors. When Christians read the Bible even now, God must reveal its meaning for their lives. Preachers claim revelations to be the source of every sermon, and when Christians are reassured through prayer, or gain some clarity about what God wants them to do, it is all credited to revelations. Everything known about Jesus, God, heaven, and hell has come through revelations.

Revelations by themselves, however, are not the whole story because Christians must discern what was revealed. Christians must believe people can consistently and reliably discern the will, behavior, and directives of an invisible, inaudible, and intangible god. But what we see, hear, and feel is subjective and vulnerable to our biases, desires, fears, social pressures, and even our current mood. The impact of subjectivity on the deeply personal experiences that constitute as revelations and discernment cannot be fully known, meaning even the most sincere and faithful Christian can be mistaken about the occurrence or meaning of a revelation.

At its root, discernment is the process of distinguishing between what comes into a person's mind naturally and what is revealed to them or impressed upon them supernaturally. Natural thought is the product of our own minds, generated from our imagination, creativity, emotions, memories, psychological disorders, and other yet-unknown biological systems. A supernatural thought, however, would need to be planted in our minds by a divine being who isn't constrained by the natural laws of our universe. Billions of people throughout human history have believed in one god or another, experiencing the presence of these gods, praying to and hearing from them. People give these gods credit for healing, work success, new cars, safety from harm, and even help finding lost keys, so their faith in these gods is bolstered by what they believe to be continued interaction and support. But to Christians, only one of these gods is real, meaning an untold number of people have believed they were impressed upon by the supernatural, but weren't.

We all have active and robust imaginations, which can cause us to think we saw or heard things that did not happen or do not exist, but Christianity requires each person to believe their mind doesn't play subversive tricks. Or that if it does, they can decipher between what is the voice or impression of

God and what is imagined. But if I believe that cult worshipers have been brainwashed by a charismatic leader, and the worshipers of false gods have been fooled by their own imagination, then some ego is required to believe I am not similarly susceptible, and that my mind, at least in this regard, is above reproach.

Although I don't agree with the characterization of humans as being "wretched, blind, and naked" as Bibles suggest, Christians are correct to distrust their own intentions. But at the same time, Christians still maintain a high sense of trust in their own abilities, which is different than the way I now see myself. I believe even a pure-hearted person is incapable of deciphering a god from his or her imagination, and Christians believe no man is pure hearted. As a Christian, I was taught the human condition is getting worse, and our minds and hearts are inherently perverted and corrupt. My mind, however, is the lens through which I would interpret all communication with a god, so if I am wretched, how can I have any confidence in my ability to perform such an important component of my spiritual walk?

I was then forced to believe the Holy Spirit can cut through the filth and limitations of humanity to speak directly and without compromise to individuals who are willing to listen. But I now see a person who is willing to listen as also eager to hear, and eager to see or feel. And given what I know about peer pressure and our active imaginations, it no longer surprises me that this eagerness results in people truly believing they are in communication with the creator of the universe.

I have encountered a few Christians who, like me, also lack confidence in their own ability to "hear" from God, but unlike me, they show great confidence in their spiritual leaders, both past and present, to achieve this task. But what I believe to be true about myself in this regard, I also believe to be true about every human who has ever lived – no one can rightly declare that their own imagination does not play a role in what they believe to be communication with an almighty creator. I've lived long enough to see how gullible people can be. I know how easily influenced I am by information that confirms my already-held beliefs, and how active my imagination can be.

I had asked my Christian family and friends for repeatable and reliable ways to distinguish between what is imagined and what is indeed supernatural, and all their responses fell into two categories. The first is that a person will feel something different about communication with God, but there is no general agreement on what that difference will be. Some believe the soul is troubled when God speaks, others believe the soul is at peace, and yet others believe the soul is sometimes troubled and sometimes at peace. This vagueness provides no instructive value to me because it sounds so similar to "You'll just know." But worshipers of false gods clearly do not just know. So, here again, if I really see myself as no more capable or incorruptible than worshipers of false gods, I cannot reasonably expect to just know when a real god is speaking.

The second set of opinions revolve around the belief that we can practice becoming better at interpreting signs and hearing still small voices. But God never offered to directly confirm or deny anyone's discernment, so what feedback informs Christians that what they discerned is correct or incorrect, or is nearly correct with some revisions? Many people can learn to interpret real-world events into a narrative which suggests their own awareness and success in communicating with the unseen. We see this used outside of Christianity to great effect by clairvoyants such as psychic mediums and tarot card readers. Through practice, though, Christians do not become any more accurate in their predictions than charlatans and worshipers of other invisible gods, nor do they exhibit any greater peace of mind, will power, or moral acumen. This is because practice needs accurate and reliable feedback, which is something Christians do not have access to.

When confronted with these challenges to the efficacy of revelations and discernment, what I've encountered from many Christians is less of a solid belief in these processes, and more of a comfortable disinterest in thinking deeply about them. Many Christians are content to say that even though they don't know how God does it, they know he can. Or that even though they don't know how they recognize the voice of God, they just do. There is little to no dispute over the problems with discernment I've presented here, but so many Christians are content to believe in what seems downright improbable as an exercise of their faith. But I now see that the faith required to believe in revelations and discernment is really a belief in our own ability to somehow do correctly what so many other billions of people, other Christians even, have done incorrectly.

It can be difficult to convince a Christian that their interactions, or the interactions of their spiritual leaders, with God have most likely been subverted by subjective bias. Nearly every Christian is comfortable in their own understanding of what Christianity is supposed to be, and can insist that their interactions with God confirm this understanding. And by being able to discount anyone else's revelation, each Christian gets to maintain that God has only really spoken to those whom they agree with, or whom they at least don't staunchly disagree with. They can do this because revelations aren't evident. So, it can be easy to look at others and suggest that these supposed Christians didn't have *real* revelations, and that they were obviously acting selfishly, prideful, or had even unintentionally misapplied scripture. These claims are made all the time by those looking to distance God from certain activities and attributes. But these attacks demonstrate that Christians already understand a key problem: revelations and discernment cannot always be trusted because they can be influenced by the individual's shortcomings. If character flaws can sabotage the process of hearing God, then it's unrealistic to expect that billions of people will be able to reliably do this. Even just expecting all the Biblical authors to have correctly navigated this process is idealistic.

Christians aren't wrong to challenge other Christians who present potentially conflicting revelations, but they *are* wrong for not confronting the way their own character issues and limited competency can invalidate their own revelations. The process of hearing from God and learning about him through revelations and discernment is mistake prone because it is so dependent on subjective experiences, but all processes that involve humans are vulnerable for this exact same reason. We need tools to help us identify and correct mistakes, but after 2,000 years, Christianity has failed to produce these tools, or to even make incremental progress toward them. In fact, I've never even been part of a substantive discussion with Christians about the need for such tools.

Without a way to test revelations, of course suicidal cults will continue to exist, and of course people will make extremely poor personal decisions based on everyday events they mistakenly interpret as signs from the almighty God. The sick will continue flocking to unscrupulous faith healers, consenting adults will continue to feel guilty about having sex outside of marriage, and poor church goers will continue "sowing a seed" by putting their rent money in the offering plate. All these things will continue to happen based on what people believe in their heart to be the voice of God, with no credible mechanism to confirm or challenge what they discerned.

Just as no individual can corroborate or dispute another's revelation, neither can they verify or test their own. The highest Biblical act of faith is a man who set out to sacrifice his son on an altar, and he did so based on a conversation he had in isolation with who he believed to be the creator of the universe. Not coincidentally, this man is also credited with initiating genital mutilation in 8-day-old boys, a practice which has lasted for thousands of years. If a Christian felt impressed to murder their own son today, or to genitally mutilate their daughter, how could they test that revelation? How can a person know if the voice is truly supernatural, or something imagined, falsely remembered, or the product of deeper psychological issues?

If it is God's plan to communicate with us telepathically while never being seen or heard in an evident way, and if we are to rely on subjective experiences for discernment, then the vast number of God-fearing and Bible-based churches in disagreement with each other should have been fully expected. New denominations form when groups of Christians hear opposing messages from God and have no way to reconcile their differences. This is essentially the ministry of Jesus Christ, as told in Bibles. His mother, father, and aunt claimed to have revelations about him being the Messiah, and he set out to convince the Jews of this. But they largely rejected him, choosing instead to lean upon their own discernment and the discernment of their forefathers, so the followers of Jesus created their own religion.

Instead of a discussion about how difficult it would have been for an entire nation to first see themselves as wrong, and second, to discern that Jesus was right in declaring himself the Messiah, I was taught the Jews who didn't accept Jesus Christ were stubborn, self-indulgent, and power hungry. These are personal attacks which, again, reveal that Christians already understand the vulnerability of revelations and discernment to our character and competency, and their problematic relationships with wrongness.

There are at least 60 Christian denominations in the United States alone, and significant tensions and disagreements within these groups continue to threaten even further divisions. This is all due to irreconcilable revelations and our inability to see our subjective experiences as not totally accurate. I grew up in a church whose fundamental differences from other religions are the belief that the original Sabbath was never moved from the 7th day of the week, Saturday, and an interpretation of Biblical prophecy which suggests we are now living in the end times before the second coming of Jesus Christ. We accepted these truths by discerning revelations and set out to convince others that their discernment was wrong and ours was right. But what tools did we hope people would use to see themselves as wrong? More subjective experiences? More prayer and Bible study? More discernment?

Most of my friends and family practice a moderate and loving iteration of Christianity and would never consider their religious views to be dangerous. But the most peace-loving Christians are bound to the most hate-filled Christians, since both groups must believe in and promote the efficacy of revelations and discernment, although each regards the other as the most damning evidence for the vulnerability of these practices. When a Christian claims to have successfully overcome their own biases to clearly hear a message from God, or claims that the dozens of Biblical authors regularly achieved this feat, this dangerously empowers others to believe they are similarly capable.

If this nebulous plan is the best an all-knowing and all-powerful god can come up with, then the floundering and sometimes problematic beliefs of Christians aren't entirely their fault, but his. Christians are essentially trying to build something meaningful and life supporting on what amounts to subjective bias. I can no longer be confident in what I learn about God through revelations and discernment. And further, be so confident that I am willing to submit my will to him, give money to his earthly agents, tell the world about him, and lean on him for joy, peace, and strength.

Atheist Marriage

I had often heard that Christ must be at the center of a marriage for it to be successful. This made sense because I had also been taught that humans are innately selfish, and the only way to overcome this selfishness in a way that is conducive to a successful marriage is through Jesus Christ. This logic came crashing down when I met an Atheist couple that had been happily married for over 20 years. They obviously had chosen *not* to make Jesus the center of their individual lives, nor the center of their marriage, yet hadn't doomed their marriage with rampant selfishness.

In response to this couple's happiness, some Christians evoke what seems to be a rehearsed skepticism that *true* happiness exists outside of Christianity. Yes, the couple could be faking their joy, but so too could Christian couples who profess happiness in Jesus. Even if this one couple was faking, though, surely Christians cannot believe there are no Atheist, Buddhist, Hindu, or Muslim couples who have enjoyed a lengthy and happy marriage. Surely there are successful non-Christian marriages, however one defines success.

If so, this means Jesus isn't *needed* to have a successful marriage. The idea of needing Jesus is hyperbole, then, and I suspect most Christians would agree about this. I think most Christians would go on to suggest that although not needed, a relationship with Jesus makes marriage, and life beyond, a whole lot easier. Hyperbole isn't unique to Christianity, or even religions, so this isn't especially problematic to me. But meeting this Atheist couple caused me to wonder how much hyperbole existed in my other beliefs about Jesus. If he isn't needed for a successful marriage, is he needed to be a good parent? Is he needed for peace of mind? Is he absolutely needed for anything at all? And this question came up at a time when I was meeting all types of religious and non-religious people who had peace of mind, joy, hope, prosperity, humility, intellect, and of course, happy marriages.

So, if I didn't need Jesus, why should I want him? Asking this question for the first time felt strange, but now necessary. I could easily find dozens of people for whom Christianity seemed to be working well, regardless of any definition of success. But when I stepped back and viewed larger groups of Christians, the answer to my question wasn't so clear. Growing up Christian, there was no doubt in my mind that Jesus was *the* pathway to the self-improvement and lifestyle I sought. Soon after meeting the Atheist couple, I now saw Jesus as *a* pathway toward those things.

My eyes were opened to the reality that happiness, love, and success are not monopolized by any particular belief system. I had been conditioned to believe my faith was the best way, and perhaps the only truly fulfilling way to navigate life's challenges. But seeing this couple live out a joyful and harmonious relationship without Jesus at the center made me reevaluate the exclusivity of what I had been taught.

This wasn't a crisis of faith for me, but rather an invitation to broaden my understanding of humanity. It reminded me that people – regardless of their beliefs – are capable of extraordinary love, compassion, and growth. The more I encountered others whose lives were filled with peace and purpose outside of Christianity, the more I questioned why I should continue believing that Jesus was the only answer.

What experiences have exposed you to humanity in a new way, and expanded your understanding of who we are or what we're capable of?

Chapter 06

A Bible

The Christian denomination I was raised in published their 28 fundamental beliefs in a long form book, and their very first stated belief is that The Bible is the word of God. The reason for stating this belief first is that all the following beliefs are supported by Bible texts, so it was important to establish the authority of these texts up front. Christians aren't allowed to believe things that simply make sense or sound true. Every belief needs to be founded in some biblical principle, but I take issue here with one particular Christian belief that has absolutely no Biblical support. In fact, this belief contradicts a plain and literal interpretation of scripture.

First, I want to make the point that there is no such thing as "the Bible." Walk into a bookstore and ask where the Bible is. Once you get to the isle, clarify that you don't just want any Bible, you want THE Bible. This may seem like a trivial exercise, but "the" is a definite article, which suggests only one. But the reality is that anyone can produce a translation, remove verses or whole books, add a couple chapters, change the commandments, or do whatever manipulation they want and still call it a bible, and still refer to it as the word of God.

Many Protestants have never heard of the Douay-Rheims translation of the bible, of which I'm not completely sure of the pronunciation because only recently was I made aware of its existence. This version was released by the Catholic church shortly before King James released his version. King James and the pope didn't see eye to eye, so King James created the Church of England, of which he was the head, murdered a bunch of Catholics in England, and decided to produce his own translation. Today, many Catholics don't read the King James Version and instead opt for the Douay-Rheims when they want the old English. Likewise, many protestants do not read the Douay-Rheims. Aside from numerous differences in the translation, the Douay-Rheims version contains First and Second Maccabees, which are not included in the current King James Version.

Rather than look into the history of how Bibles came to be, many Christians faithfully believe that what is in their bible is what God wants them to have, however it got there. This suggests that God actively guided the development and translation of the scriptures. But did God protect both the Catholic and Protestant versions equally? Do all bibles at the bookstore hold in them exactly what God intends for their readers to have? What about the Bibles given to enslaved African Americans two hundred years ago, from which texts were taken out that might have inspired an uprising? Did those Bibles have in them exactly what God wanted them to have?

It's important to create a distinction here, because what people say they believe about "the" Bible, they only believe about some bibles. When people talk about the Bible, they really mean "their" Bibles – the Bibles sitting in their home, that their parents used, and that their minister preaches from. They believe *these* Bibles have been protected by God, but not those sitting in Catholic homes, not the Bibles sitting in Mormon homes, and presumably not the Bibles given to enslaved peoples.

But the Bible itself is full of texts extolling the virtues of "all scripture." Nowhere does it say only some scripture is God breathed. The Bible is silent regarding additions, subtractions, papal- and monarchy-driven translations. To be fair, the Bible is also silent about the internet and driving the speed limit, which is understandable because those things didn't exist. But when the New Testament books were written, there were many versions of almost every Old Testament book floating around Judea, yet the Biblical authors still chose words such as "all" and "every" when reporting about scripture.

Ask a religious leader in a Protestant denomination for clarification on a text from First Maccabees and they will likely say that book isn't a part of the authorized canon. Follow up by asking where God authorized some books and not others, or authorized King James but not Douay-Rheims? The answer will not be Biblical, which is supposed to be a problem. Excluding Maccabees goes against a plain and literal interpretation of scripture. Excluding the Apocrypha, which was included in King James' original translation, goes against a plane and literal translation of scripture. But this is all accepted practice.

Once the literal interpretation of these texts about "all scripture" is tossed aside, the challenge then becomes deciding which scripture is God breathed, and which isn't. This opens the door for some believers to suggest that the central theme of the Bible, God is love, has been protected regardless of which translation is read. In fact, this was the underlying concept laid out by the church of my youth as their first "fundamental" belief. But this results in another problematic question, which parts of Bibles are included in this underlying harmony, and which are superfluous? Because if only the underlying harmony was protected, then should the other texts be revered as God breathed?

I've heard Christians say the Holy Spirit convicted them of which Bible to use and which texts of their Bible are God breathed, and of course these events cannot be corroborated because revelations and discernment are deeply personal events. But I've never heard a Protestant feel convicted that the Douay Rheims version is God's authorized text, and I've never heard a Catholic say God protected the King James

Version. This begs the question of whether tradition or conviction is at work here, since tradition is one of the pathways for subjective bias to influence our spiritual beliefs.

Bible readers often like to insulate themselves from questions like these, choosing to believe their Bible is the word of God, and avoiding any thought toward what other people are reading in their Bibles. The popular refrains "I'm just worried about what God gave to me" and "I'm not to worry about other people's spiritual lives and salvation" are used to justify a myopic view of this issue. So much so that this type of Biblical thoughtlessness and refusal to ask broad questions masquerades as high faith.

Lacking is a broad and consistent narrative about God's role as the originator and protector of certain scripture throughout time. I am old enough to remember many Christians teaching that only the King James Version has been protected by God, a belief itself which has no Biblical support, but one that now almost no one believes. What changed? Who was wrong? And did that wrongness inform Christians about how to better understand and clarify what appears in Bibles exactly as God intended? No, believers and denominations are still just as vulnerable to subjectivity as they attempt to arbitrate issues of Biblical inspiration.

If God wrote and protected a particular passage of scripture, it would simply be unfortunate for a believer to dismiss those texts because of some uncertainty about their origin. But the converse – believing God authored texts he had nothing to do with – is terribly dangerous. Because once "thus saith the Lord" is attached to a text and interpretation, it becomes impossible to refute. This isn't an area where widespread ambiguity should be acceptable, but this is what exists throughout Christianity. There is a general lack of consensus about what God wrote and protected, and what he didn't.

But this is not the only issue with Bibles. Even if the Christian god is real and had a hand in authoring the Bible such that certain passages of scripture appear exactly the way he intended, through its authorship and translation, there are still a few challenges to understanding the intended message. Three questions must be asked of any Biblical passage to determine how it should be interpreted for those living 2,000 years after the book was finished.

1) Who is the speaker? Is it the physical author of the passage, or is God the speaker and the author was simply the pen?

2) Is there relevant context, and is the speaker using a figure of speech or being literal? Is the passage an allegory or an actual historical event?

3) Who is the audience? Is the author speaking to an individual, a city, his religious group, or to all humanity for all

time? Or do passages have multiple meanings for multiple audiences?

I don't know what is taught in theological seminaries, but these are the three questions I find appropriate to ask when interpreting scripture.

Some believers read the Bible having already decided the character and personality of God. All texts are either interpreted by these individuals to support that version of God or put aside as something we cannot yet understand. Using this approach, scripture is interpreted or understood based on what is already known about God. There are others, however, who do not start with a preconceived notion of who God is, and they hope to learn about him based upon what is written in their Bible. But once the assumptions about God's perfect character are removed, the process of interpreting texts becomes less trivial. Just like I was handed an idea of the Christian god by my parents, they also taught me how to interpret several critical texts to support this version of God. In certain texts, the speaker is God and he is speaking literally to every person that will ever live. In other texts, Paul is speaking figuratively to the leaders of a particular church. Some stories are parables, and other stories are factual accounts.

Many Christians believe God is against homosexuality, due largely to certain speaker-audience interpretations of a few texts in both the Old and New Testament. It had become important for me to learn about how Jesus feels about homosexuality and homosexuals, because wanting homosexuals to die, at any point in history, does not seem of high morality. Leviticus literally says that homosexuality is an abomination, and many followers of Christ suggest the audience for that text is all of humanity for all time. But the text also asserts that men engaging in homosexuality should be put to death, a part of the verse that almost no Christians still believe they are to obey. I find it difficult to believe God was speaking to all of humanity in one part of the verse, but only to the children of Israel in another part of the verse. There is a consistency problem here, and the way I was taught to interpret Bibles is full of these kinds of issues.

In the New Testament, Paul says homosexuality is unnatural. Is Paul, a fallible and non-scientist human being, the speaker, or is God the speaker? Chapters later, Paul says women should be quiet in church, but no one really interprets that to be the voice of God speaking to all humanity for all time. Instead, many read that as Paul speaking about certain unlearned women in a certain church. On the surface, it is inconsistent to say God is the speaker in one chapter, but Paul is the speaker in the next chapter; and God was speaking to all humanity in one chapter, but it was only Paul speaking to people of that time in the next chapter. This inconsistency is often resolved by incorporating a larger goal, such as the desire to confirm that God is good. This allows Christians to make the human author responsible for complicated texts, and credit God for the texts they want to have power exactly as written.

One of Jesus' parables is about a rich man who died and was being tormented in Hades, but asked Abraham, who was some kind of gatekeeper in the afterlife, if he could warn his living brothers to live a better life. Some Bible readers don't believe people go directly to hell after they die, or that dead people can communicate with the living, so how do they reconcile their beliefs with this story? Quite easily, they assume the events in the story did not literally occur, but that the sole purpose of the parable was simply to teach a lesson. In fact, the ministry of Jesus is full of parables, so this was obviously a tool Biblical authors found valuable.

So, could the creation story also be figurative, and have been written simply to teach a lesson? The story which had talking snakes and magical trees was interpreted as purely literal in my childhood home and church, but Science and History are mounting increasing evidence to the contrary. Did Jesus really allow Satan to kill all of Job's children to prove a point? Did Jesus tell the Children of Israel to commit genocide? Does Jesus really believe women should be quiet in church? Does God dislike mixed fabrics more than he dislikes slavery?

The point here is not a defense of evolution or homosexuality, but to make clear that answering interpretive questions differently can lead to drastically differing conclusions about the character of Christ. And I have never seen nor heard a consistent approach to answering the three interpretive questions that does not rely on a personal revelation or the pre-accepted conclusion that God is perfect. Every Bible-based religion and denomination in the world started the same way: a prophet or Biblical scholar, Jesus included, challenged an interpretation of scripture, but that person didn't have enough authority nor a formal process by which to validate their new interpretation of scripture, so the individual had to start a new church with whatever group of believers they could convince. When conflicting views of God are compared side by side though, the varying beliefs are all due to differing answers to the three previously mentioned questions for a relatively small number of texts. Who is the speaker? Is the speaker being literal? Who is the audience?

Catholics don't dunk their new converts underwater because they believe the baptism commands to be figurative. Jews don't pay tithe because they interpret literally and for all time the command to only pay tithe to Levites. Seventh-Day Sabbath keepers believe the 4th commandment was not just spoken to the Children of Israel, but to all people for all time. It is important to have clarity about these concepts since they address the way in which Christ wants his followers to operate until he returns. Perhaps the most interesting difference in interpretation is of the texts in Old Testament Malachi which explicitly state that Elijah will return when the Jewish Messiah returns. Followers of Jesus Christ insist this text be read figuratively, and that John the Baptist was the symbolic version of Elijah. Jesus is said to have even alluded to this. Many Jews, however, interpreted the Malachi passage literally and so rejected Jesus as the Christ, and still wait for the return of Elijah and their Messiah. As a child, I learned that Jews rejected Jesus as the Christ because of the hardness of their hearts, and they wanted to hold onto power. And perhaps some did, but many were standing by a literal and plain interpretation of scripture. It is not entirely clear that Christians who now preach that the Bible is clearly written and should be interpreted literally would have accepted Jesus when he walked the earth, since doing so would have required figurative interpretations.

Followers of Christ are no better prepared to handle issues of Biblical interpretation now than thousands of years ago when this man named Jesus claimed to be God in the flesh, and asked people to accept an alternative interpretation of several key scriptures. He basically asked Jews to accept that they had been wrong about scripture for thousands of years, but Jews had no mechanism to correct their beliefs, other than the same subjective processes that yielded the beliefs they already held. And all these years later, there are still no straightforward and consistent processes for interpreting scripture outside of revelations, which are vulnerable to tradition and other subjective influences.

Multiple religious organizations are trying to decide if women should be ordained ministers, and both sides of this debate have Bible texts, well-respected preachers, and scholars supporting their position. Growing up Christian, I learned that when a person prays for guidance before studying the Bible, God will help them to understand what is written. In the case of ordaining women though, many individuals pray and search the scriptures, then arrive at different conclusions. All the individuals feel as though their Bible study was led by God, but one side of this debate is wrong. Not only wrong on the issue, but also wrong in the belief that their god guided them. Unless God is leading people to two opposing conclusions, it must be conceded that at least one side of this debate hasn't heard from God at all, despite their belief to the contrary and their earnest prayers for guidance. Because Biblical interpretation relies on personal revelations, all the subjective issues problematic with that process apply here as well.

It seems reasonable to ask how so many people who think they've been led by the Holy Spirit keep coming up with conflicting conclusions. One person says, "God is the speaker in these texts, and these texts are figurative, and this text is meant for all people for all time," and then another person says, "No, Paul is speaking literally only to those people at that time." Individuals cannot be sure they've been led by the spirit and not by their own ideas about what the Bible says. It's too easy to start with a conclusion and then answer the interpretive questions to have the Bible also reach that same conclusion.

Many Christians speak with great certainty about their interpretation of scripture but present no consistent and objective mechanism for how they arrived at that interpretation. Before anyone can convince me of *what* they have interpreted from scripture, I need to be convinced about *how* they have interpreted scripture, and that their method isn't prone to confirmation bias.

Credibility is lost when answers to the interpretive questions change within the same verse, or from one chapter to the next. But without a systematic approach to interpretation, individuals can get stuck in fallacies without a way out. I read through the predictions of one prophet, Harold Camping, and the dates which led him to believe the second coming would be in 2011. As can be guessed, his numbers add up. Some literal interpretation here, some figurative interpretation there, and… wallah! All of Christendom used to believe the Sun rotates around the Earth because of a literal interpretation of Bible texts that say the Earth sits still. When Christians finally admitted the scientists were correct, there was no accompanying process outlined to avoid this type of interpretive mistake in the future. And sadly, none still exists outside of asking for guidance from the Holy Spirit.

Well-intentioned people can make mistakes, which is why objectivity is so necessary. The sheer number of disagreeing Bible-based religions in the world confirms this lack of objectivity in Biblical interpretation. The same Bible used to support slavery was also used to support its abolition, and the same Bible used to preach peace can also be used to incite violence. I cannot operate this way. I cannot get up from Bible study and wonder if the Holy Spirit guided my study, or if I just arrived at the conclusions that my biased subconscious sought out.

Reason to Stay

I was losing my grasp on the Christian faith. I wanted to remain Christian, but the idea seemed more and more untenable. The belief system was intellectually difficult to maintain, so I tried for another motivation: Was it useful?

I began asking my Christian friends and family to name three ways they benefit from their faith because I was hoping one of them would give me a reason to stay. Almost every person mentioned the hope heaven provides. Some were interested in reuniting with loved ones, and others looked forward to seeing Jesus. Primarily people felt comforted to know all the pain and suffering here on Earth had a purpose and would ultimately come to an end.

Some people spoke about peace of mind, others valued an explanation for suffering in the world, and a few appreciated the sense of community offered by Christian fellowship. Of these, community was the most significant to me. Nearly all my family and friends were Christian, so walking away from the faith would change the dynamic of many of these relationships. I never looked forward to heaven, even at the height of my spiritual connection, because it happened in the afterlife. The explanation for suffering also was never valuable to me, mostly because I knew God could end all the suffering by coming back, and the reasons I had been given for him not returning yet didn't make much sense to me. We surely didn't need thousands of years of suffering for any good-versus-evil point to be made.

In the end, my search for reasons to remain Christian led me to pursue a deeper understanding of what I truly valued from my belief systems. I still haven't answered that question fully, but I've come to accept that Christianity no longer serves me. I'm left with the realization that belief should resonate deeply with who I am, and if it doesn't, it's okay to let it go and keep searching. And so, I did.

What is it that you seek from your belief systems? Are they a source of truth, meaning, comfort, certainty, or a guide for how you engage with the world, or something else entirely?

Chapter 07

Prophecy

Fulfilled prophecy is touted as evidence the Bible was inspired by an all-knowing and supernatural being. Indeed, if such prophecies existed, they would provide a strong case for the existence of a god who knows the future and is in contact with humanity. But instead, most prophecies are vague, ambiguous, and only interpreted after the predicted events occur. In instances where a prophecy has been interpreted to predict a future event, but nothing evident occurs, the interpretation or the interpreters are typically blamed rather than the prophecy itself. The most lasting prophecies are too vague to ever be contradicted by any observable events, or the lack thereof. And these vague prophecies can be interpreted and re-interpreted to describe 100 different events, but they will never be wrong.

Just as the Christian god has chosen not to make himself directly observable, he has apparently chosen not to make his prophecies objectively clear. And just as Christians disagree about what their god is doing or has done, they also disagree about what messages their god has given through prophecy. As a young Christian, I was taught the Biblical prophecies written in the books of Daniel and Revelations. The specific interpretations of these prophecies were much easier to believe when they were the only ones I was aware of, and when I had full confidence in those teaching me. I have since come across other interpretations of these prophecies that are equally convoluted in that they require the reader to accept some associations and connections that are not entirely straightforward. Prophesies "hidden" in symbols are effectively useless to those like me who seek objectivity, since the problems previously described regarding Biblical interpretation and hearing from a supernatural being apply to the interpretations of any ambiguous prophecies. The interpretation of prophecies is also largely a solitary experience, so it is easily influenced by bias and the desires of the interpreter.

It is not entirely clear who wrote the prophetic chapters in the book of Daniel, or when they were written. I had once accepted that the texts in Daniel were written many thousands of years ago, long before the events predicted in the texts, and were unmodified through transcription and translation. But it is entirely possible that parts of the prophecies were written or edited *after* major events occurred, and then attributed to Daniel to provide the appearance of a prediction. Further, the exact year of Rome's demise was supposedly predicted by Daniel thousands of years before it happened, but this prophecy was not interpreted by anyone until several centuries after Rome had fallen. This is largely due to the vagueness of the prophecy, which is so problematic that it still isn't clear even among Christians that the author of Daniel was referring to the fall of Rome. There is no question the beasts and horns mentioned in the prophecy are all figurative, and by proclaiming to be a prophet, Daniel claims to speak on behalf of God, but deciphering what each object represents has caused a great deal of disagreement and confusion.

As for the prophecies in the book of Revelations, and other forward-looking texts like those which appear in the Gospels, again there is a great deal of symbolism that must be interpreted to determine what is being predicted. Other oft-cited, end-time predictions mention the occurrence of earthquakes in diverse places, along with wars and rumors of wars, but there has never been a time in the 2,000 years since these texts were written that there weren't earthquakes in diverse places, wars, and rumors of wars. I am not aware of any widely accepted specific predictions from Revelations that have occurred. There are subgroups of believers who connect texts to relatively recent events, such as the establishment of Israel in 1948, but the language in these prophecies is so obscure that only a small percentage of even Bible-believing Christians can agree about what is being described. I have asked many of my Christian friends for the last observable event to occur that was predicted by scripture, and the next event expected to occur. I have never received an answer, but I won't be surprised when a major global event occurs, and these same friends claim that it had been predicted plainly and clearly by the Bible.

Modern-day prophets also fail to provide clear and unambiguous predictions that come true with any regularity. Some claim to illuminate the past through insight which cannot be corroborated. Descriptions of heaven also cannot be verified, for obvious reasons. A prophet who much of my family takes seriously claimed in the 1800s to have been shown two moons of Jupiter on a voyage through the solar system. This was exactly the number of moons known to scientists at the time, but since then, many more moons have been located. How powerful would it have been if the prophet saw all the moons *before* scientists discovered them? How easy would it have been for an all-knowing God, who created these moons, to show them to his prophet in correct detail?

I am not making conclusive statements about all prophets and prophecies being wrong, nor am I saying anyone who believes in them has been misled. I am only describing why these kinds of prophecies have no value in *my* life. I previously wondered why a god who knows everything about the future would only communicate parts of it so vaguely to his believers. I've heard multiple explanations from Christians as to why God chose this approach to prophecy, but now I have accepted that if God exists, for whatever reason, he isn't going to change any time soon – this is his way. If these prophecies were given by a supernatural being to draw other people to Christ, then they have surely succeeded, but they do not pass my test for credibility.

The vagueness and ambiguity of Christian prophecies leave them widely open to interpretation and vulnerable to bias and wishful thinking. Here again, subjectivity reigns in the process of hearing from God. If the Christian god requires faith instead of objectivity to see and understand the prophecies he has given to his people, then they were not designed to attract or inform me.

Carlton Pearson

I don't recall how I stumbled across Bishop Carlton Pearson, but it was probably on the internet somehow. Pearson was the preacher at an evangelical Christian mega church and had been groomed by Oral Roberts to be the next big thing. He had a congregation of over 5,000 attendees long before the modern era of tele-evangelism which now sees churches of this size in almost every major city.

Bishop Pearson arrived at church one Sunday and told his congregation that every person who has ever lived is going to heaven, and hell is what we put each other through here on Earth. He argued, from Biblical texts of course, that the blood of Jesus is sufficient to cover *all* sins. His congregation wasn't convinced and attendance plummeted, but Pearson's message has since resonated with a growing number of people, and a movie has been made about his revelation and journey with this new truth.

Hearing Bishop Pearson's theory was interesting to me for two reasons. First, it's ridiculous. This has nothing to do with how true or false it is, but it's very far from anything most Christians believe about the afterlife. He claims God gave this truth to him directly, which illustrates the malleability of

Christianity. In 1,000 years, most Christians may believe in Bishop Pearson's god, or an even more generous god, or a more cruel one, each supported by scripture.

The second interesting thing about Bishop Pearson's revelation is that his god seems more loving than a god who would burn up his own children for the crime of not choosing him. I was taught the Christian god loves me far more than I could ever love my own children, but I can't imagine anything any of my children could do to make me burn them alive. That is a type of love I cannot understand and do not want, particularly if I had the ability to change my children, as many Christians believe God will change their sinful nature on the way to heaven.

I hadn't thought about hell fire as being cruel until I compared the god of my youth to Pearson's god. Burning people alive, or even burning them at all, now seemed petty and very human, not loving and aspirational. As I was losing my faith, I began to wonder if I even wanted to regain it. Do I want to worship *this* god? Many nonbelievers call the Christian god cruel, selfish, hypocritical, and egotistical, and as I began to read Bible stories with questioning eyes, the goodness of God certainly wasn't always obvious.

If Bibles are true, then the Christian god appears to have condoned rape and slavery, and commanded genocide, among other things. I am not certain if he exists or not, but I was becoming thankful the evidence for him is weak. The more I thought about it, the less I wanted to worship a god whose love felt indistinguishable from cruelty.

Is it harder to believe things you don't want to be true, or does believing them to be true eliminate that difficulty?

Chapter 08

Miracles

Christians bolster their confidence in God by crediting him for interventions in their lives, particularly after they've requested him to do so. Although many people regard the rising of the sun and the advancement of technology as miraculous, most testimonies revolve around more personal acts of God's favor through an extraordinary or unexplainable experience. But because neither the Christian god nor his angels can visibly be seen performing these acts, faith is required to credit him for any good that transpires.

Gods of all religions, both past and present, have received credit for what occurs in the lives of their believers because our minds can so easily be convinced that because one event precedes another, it played some role in causing the successive event. If a person prays for a new job and gets hired, many Christians are trained to believe the prayer caused God to act, which led to the new job.

After over 30 years of hearing my family and friends make these kinds of causal assumptions, it was easy for me to make these connections as well. And the idea of a personal god is born out of this notion that my prayers can move him to perform miracles. Through answered prayers, Christians understand their god to be attentive to their needs, and many believe God has a protective hedge around their family or group of believers.

Causal errors occur not just regarding religious truth, but in all pursuits of knowledge such as astronomy, psychology, and history. These errors are so pervasive because it's a shortcut our minds like to take, even when there is insufficient support. And once a person accepts a belief, even one with flimsy or poor support, they often require a mountain of evidence to change their minds. This is not the way any belief in the affirmative should work. A person's belief in an idea should be proportionate to the supporting evidence, not to the lack of disproving evidence. The belief that God is performing miracles should be based on some evidence to that fact, not the lack of evidence to disprove it. Like everyone, I accept some things to be true which cannot be experimentally proven in a laboratory. But I do not then require double-blind, peer-reviewed, and pastor-approved research studies to rethink my position.

Bibles suggest faith is the evidence of things not seen, so Christians need not see their god acting to have evidence of him doing so. Their faith suffices. The problem is that praying people and non-praying people both have all the same things and don't have the same things. Praying people don't have more of anything. And this doesn't just include tangible things like big houses and fancy cars, but also peace of mind, joy, and hope, and undesirable things such as sexual abuse, suicide, and divorce. Belief in the power of prayer suggests that people who don't pray are without this power, or without miracles. The Bible acknowledges that bad things will happen to good people, and vice versa, but as a child I believed in the connection between what we asked God for and what he did for us. I believed the Christian god was blessing our family through miraculous intervention, and his angels were protecting us from danger seen and unseen. It seemed natural then to believe that those who didn't make these requests of God through prayer weren't being equally blessed nor protected. It took many years to realize that the sum of the miracles we claimed to receive from God did not result in a life much different than that of the Catholics, Buddhists, and Atheists I have met.

The most sincere and heartfelt prayers I have heard in my life, where people have pleaded with God for a miracle, have been in advocacy of someone with cancer. But Christians who pray neither have less incidents of cancer than the general population, nor more instances of recovery. And no person, prayed for or not, has regrown an amputated limb. And no person born with Down syndrome, prayed for or not, has lost the effects of the extra chromosome. These were powerful realities to accept while still maintaining my belief in a personal god, so my idea of the Christian god shifted to eliminate the connection between prayer and miracles. I still had faith that God *could* perform miracles, but that he rarely did, particularly in response to prayer. I didn't know anyone who had a good understanding of when or why only certain prayers would lead to healing. Christians seem comfortable to accept God answers prayers according to his will, but because no one knows what his will is, there is no way to align our prayers to it.

I had stopped praying for God to provide myself or others with cars, job promotions, or physical healing. Instead, I prayed for peace of mind, strength in adversity, or comfort to a loved one. I know many Christians who also pray this way, perhaps believing like I did that these less-observable requests are more likely to be granted. But this idea of prayer and the Christian god does not agree with the Bible stories in which requests for tangible and observable intervention were granted, sometimes in spectacular ways. I had rationalized that the Christian god acts differently now than he did then.

These requests for personal and emotional interventions have the added feature of not being objectively observable. Even when a believer achieves peace of mind, there is an ambiguous causal relationship between that peace of mind and any preceding prayer. This is because peace of mind amid adversity is not exclusively observed among Christians, nor does peace of mind seem to be granted whenever it's asked of the Christian god. The miracle of peace of mind, comfort, strength, joy, hope, and other desirable emotions are much like the healing of cancer in that there are no perceivable relationships to prayer beyond what can be seen through faith.

People often assume causation has occurred when a correlation is observed. In this case, a correlation would exist if cancer or mental health issues were less prevalent in Christians than the general population. But causation still couldn't be proved until other potential causes such as diet and community socialization were investigated. But incidents of cancer and other illnesses are *not* lower among Christians, meaning Christians must be willing to accept a causal relationship between their prayers and any succeeding miracles even when a correlation doesn't exist.

It is understandably difficult for a person to avoid the causal trap when they pray for healing, or are prayed for, and then subsequently recover. This situation provides the appearance of a correlation and perhaps causation, but only when viewed in isolation. When this apparent healing is viewed in the context of even five others in the same family, same hospital, or same church community who were also prayed for, the lack of correlation becomes clear, and causation is impossible to substantiate objectively. This is why Christians must value personal and individual experiences taken in isolation, and either disregard or flat out ignore others who weren't healed, to maintain the belief that prayers lead to miraculous medical recoveries. Even wild and abnormal recoveries which cannot be explained by doctors must be viewed in context. I know Christians who have been at the center of these recoveries, and they cannot be dissuaded out of their belief that God's miraculous intervention is responsible for their healing, but this is the acceptance of evidence by faith, which too often disagrees with a more objective view of facts.

The connection between prayer and miracles can only be seen through the lens of faith, which makes Christianity similarly unremarkable when compared to all other religions. If faith, a deeply personal feeling, is the only means by which humans can recognize the hand of God moving in their lives, then the process is prone to biases and preconceived notions about what God would and would not do. But even the most ardent Christian must admit they don't fully know what God would do because they don't know the mind of God. This is a problematic way to build a belief system because it's based on our subjective understanding of the things we and others have experienced. Because we cannot see God, we can completely discredit his contributions or even attribute his works to other gods. All of this makes the recognition of miracles a highly unreliable pathway to truth or an understanding of what is real and what is not.

Reclaiming the Bible

The book "Reclaiming the Bible for a Non-Religious World" by John Shelby Spong proved to be the final nail in my Christian coffin. When this book came into my life, I was hanging onto Christianity by a thread. But I didn't know what to do with the Bible because I still found it to be an amazing collection of awe-inspiring stories that has been relevant for over 2,000 years. Even if it wasn't infallible, and even if there were questions about its authorship and interpretation, I still considered it to be uniquely special and quite possibly divinely inspired in some way.

Spong combined what's *in* Bibles with historical information about that period to tell the story *of* Bibles. He presented an alternate way to view the Bible, outside of literal truth and supernatural intervention. He believed most sermons and Bible studies focus on the same small set of stories, and much of what's in the Bible isn't known to most Christians. I had gone to Christian schools all my life and had taken the Bible very seriously for much of that time, but Spong pointed out pertinent details in parts of the Bible I had not read, or did not understand.

He showed that the Old Testament can be seen as stories written by Jewish religious leaders to hold the nation together, and to bolster their sense of self. He suggested that facts and literal truth may not have been as important as the desired message to be conveyed. His alternate view of the New Testament described it as a tool used by early Christians seeking to convert the Romans around them.

Re-reading familiar texts in this context provided an explanation for so many of the problems I had with the Bible. The errors, contradictions, and confusion now had a very straightforward explanation. All I had known was the supernatural explanation for what Bibles contain and how they came to be, and "Reclaiming the Bible" provided a non-supernatural explanation which seemed far more plausible.

Almost everything we know about the Christian God originates with Bibles. If we can learn about God through nature, it is only because Bibles have told us God is directly responsible for nature. If we can learn about God through our experiences with him, it is only because Bibles have shown us how God interacts with humanity. And so now that I see Bibles as wholly man made, with all the pitfalls of that distinction, I had nothing else in Christianity to hold on to.

Even before finishing "Reclaiming the Bible," I knew my last tie to Christianity had been severed. I didn't have the heart to ever finish the book, as the reality of my deconversion set in, and reading further seemed like piling on. I closed the book, and said to myself, "I'm done." And from that day forward, I haven't called myself a Christian.

What titles or labels have been difficult for you to let go of?

Chapter 09

Value

Belief in the Christian god, like belief in all other gods, resides
in a space of uncertainty. No scientist can disprove the
Christian god's existence, and no Christian can prove their
god's existence. All unprovable and un-disprovable ideas
should not be treated equally, however, as some ideas have
more support than others, and some ideas have been more
valuable than others. Many persons and groups have
provided their own descriptions of how the universe began
and what happens after death, and while no explanation can
be absolutely proven or disproven, each can also be measured
according to its value. Can the explanation be used to
improve the lives of people by helping us to better predict or
control our own behavior, or other aspects of the natural
world?

Christians are not less likely to be homeless, catch the flu, or
even die in an unfortunate accident. There is no *observable*
value to Christianity, but Christians promote a less visible,
perhaps immeasurable, value. Christians maintain there is
value in simply believing God exists, he loves us, died for our
sins, and wants to take us to heaven. Christians derive a sense
of purpose from their faith, and in that story find an

explanation for the suffering they experience and witness. The Christian story provides a reason for the persistent strife many of us feel, and a reward for those whose faith endures. The promise of heaven and a world with no bills, no sickness, and no death is attractive to those who have experienced significant "trials and tribulations" in their lifetime.

It is said that Jesus Christ will carry our burdens if we just give them over to him. The refrain to "Let go and let God" speaks to the idea that Christians should stop worrying because their all-powerful and all-knowing god will work everything out for their good. Believing in this god is said to engender feelings of hope, peace of mind, and joy. These benefits, for some, are worth more than the need for scientific or historical corroboration, making challenges from these fields easy to ignore. I have heard a few Christians say that at the end of their lives, if they were to learn that Christianity wasn't real – that it was all made up – they wouldn't regret having been a Christian because their faith has been a source of great joy and positivity in their lives.

This is not a ridiculous perspective to have. When the scientific method is replaced by a better way to investigate phenomena and acquire new knowledge, those of us who practiced science will not regret having done so, due to what we claim to be its obvious value. Likewise, in the absence of solid evidence disproving God, Christians are happy to maintain a belief they feel benefited by. For many people, belief in Jesus Christ is predicated on value rather than their ability to prove its truth.

Christians claim their belief in Jesus Christ is a source of comfort and peace of mind, which has helped them to negotiate a world they see as cruel and only getting worse. Reuniting with loved ones who died too soon, and the promise of a "better day afterwhile" is believed to bring hope to those who have endured considerable heartache and loss. Christians claim to find purpose within their faith, and an explanation for pain and suffering. I also seek comfort, peace of mind, hope, and purpose, and want to have more compassion, charity, and gratitude toward others, and more joy, love, introspection, and humility in my own life. I had to answer for myself what *value*, if any, Christianity added to my pursuit of these goals.

Since becoming an atheist, I have been asked where morality comes from, if not from God. How do Atheists handle tragedy and account for suffering? What hope do Atheists have? The questions have been asked with true regard for my wellbeing, which may be a consequence of believing, as Bibles suggest, that godlessness equates to wickedness. But the questions are problematic because they wrongly assume there is widespread peace of mind, morality, and hope within Christianity – as if by leaving Christianity, I am losing access to these things.

When someone introduces themselves to me as Christian, though, I cannot assume anything about their feelings toward moral issues such as racism, patriarchy, abortion, the death penalty, and homosexuality. I cannot assume they give of their time or other resources to the less fortunate, nor can I assume they don't have high anxiety or constant feelings of hopelessness and despair. Christianity is so malleable that racists, freedom fighters, capitalists, pacifists, and war mongers all find justification within its tenets.

Rather than Christianity shaping the moral leanings of its practitioners, it seems that each person's sense of morality dictates which version of Christianity they embrace, and ultimately which version of the Christian god they believe in. And then by leaning on this version of God for morality and a sense of hope, peace, and joy, too many believers have only created a mirror for their own morality and their own ideals. This accounts for the wide range of moral latitude and emotional well-being within Christianity. So, just as I am asked by Christians about the sources of morality and peace of mind in Atheism, it would be equally appropriate of me to ask of my Christian friends and family what guides their morality and how they deal with pain and suffering.

I do not see awe-inspiring joy or widespread peace of mind among Christians, nor do I see pervasive hope or compassion. The reward of heaven fails to instill many Christians with enough willpower to abide by their own moral codes, although morality is defined differently from group to group, and from generation to generation. The Christian explanation for pain and suffering does not reliably curtail the emotional effects of actual pain and suffering. This is despite the often-repeated refrains that unexplainable events are part of God's plan, and that "God works in mysterious ways." An afterlife with no sickness and no sadness sounds appealing, but believing in heaven does not consistently help individuals here on Earth to overcome feelings of hopelessness and despair. Christianity suggests that life, with all its disappointments and suffering, has a greater purpose, that it all means something, but these beliefs do not produce within Christianity a more noble or well-adjusted class of people.

These realities would seem to make Christianity rather unremarkable, but throughout my own childhood and young adult years, the potential of Christianity was buoyed by the few Christians I knew whose character and demeanor exemplified *all* the qualities I desired. They gave freely of their time, energy, and money, and their understanding of scripture always bent toward helping the less fortunate and being more considerate of others. They encouraged, uplifted, sacrificed, empathized, and did just about whatever it took to make people feel loved. Their own lives were not without suffering and loss, but they coped with a sense of acceptance and resolve that inspired many others. On their deathbeds, these individuals still exhibit such a level of dignity and peace of mind that even the attending health professionals find remarkable.

A few years ago, because my circle of relationships was nearly entirely Christian, everyone I knew with this type of character and demeanor was a Christian, which made it easy to credit faith for their inspiring lives. Despite the rarity of these individuals within Christianity, they have always been one of its most effective advertisements – "*This* is what Christianity can do for you. *This* is the kind of person Christianity can help you to become." One of the primary reasons to accept the idea of the Christian god, pray to him, and try to be more like him is the perception that it works. So, these individuals make great tele-evangelists and preachers, as their "do what I do to live how I live" message resonates with people who are seeking personal growth in some aspect of their lives.

My maternal grandmother was one of these exceptional individuals and was also an extraordinary Christian. I now believe she also could have been an amazing Buddhist, Muslim, Hindu, or Jain, had she been born in the places where those religions are dominant. Just as she did within Christianity, she would have encouraged people toward the more loving tenets of whichever faith she practiced. Looking back on her life and remembering all the times she pushed against the Christian thought of her day, and how she helped to guide the spiritual journeys of so many around her, I can't help but wonder if Christianity benefited more from her than she did from it. I cannot credit Christianity for the love my grandmother exhibited. Instead, I credit my grandmother for making the Christianity I grew up into more loving.

Many Christians have seen their parents live lives of peace and joy with moments of heartache and pain, and through it all depend on a relationship with Jesus Christ. Many Christians see their friends as mostly good and associate that goodness with their Christian lifestyles. Parents, family members, and close friends explicitly sell Christianity to young people by crediting Christ and their faith in him for all the good in their lives. My parents have always attributed their joy, peace of mind, and quality of life to Jesus Christ. All their good decisions and good acts were credited to him. All their financial blessings, work promotions, and new cars became testimonies in church and family worship.

Parents are not wrong in doing this. If they view their own faith as a coping mechanism or otherwise a benefit in their lives, it makes sense for them to pass their idea of God onto their children. For many years, I operated under the assumption that if faith in the Christian god worked for my parents and grandparents, and if it's working for most of my friends, then it's good enough for me.

I have never been accused of displaying enviable levels of charity or hope, but I've also never lost a minute of sleep worrying or dealing with self-esteem issues. I am almost always in a good mood, and helping people makes me feel good. I was indoctrinated into attributing these character and personality traits to my faith in the Christian god. I believed that these and any other expressions of charity and benevolence had to be Christ working through me, because I was a selfish sinner who could only be redeemed through the brutal murder of a man god.

Like many children raised in Christian homes, I became serious about my faith and spiritual walk in middle and high school. As I matured, what nonbelievers would describe as normal human development, I regarded as growth in Christ. Through the lens of Christianity, becoming more responsible and thinking about my future were both signs that Christ was in my life. There was such a chorus of affirmation toward Christianity by the family members and friends who raised me that I never considered whether Christianity was really working in people's lives. In my teenage years, I didn't have close friends from other religions, so I had no way of comparing Christianity to anything else. It wasn't clear to me then how passionately Buddhists claim their teachings work, and how fervently Atheists suggest that rejecting all gods works. So, for me, living in this Christian echo chamber, it became second nature to credit Christianity for all the good in my life.

The problem with attributing all the good in our lives to Christianity is that Christians do not have a monopoly on benevolence, prosperity, or peace of mind. I previously believed that by not acknowledging the giver of peace, non-Christians rarely found long-lasting happiness or joy. It also seemed reasonable to believe that if Christ forms a hedge around those who trust in him, then nonbelievers have no such hedge. These ideas were instilled into me as the value of Christianity, and I couldn't know this as a child because of my narrow view of the world, but people of almost every major belief system manifest the qualities I seek. The older I get, and the wider my circle of friends and acquaintances becomes, the more clearly I see this truth.

How can Christianity be credited for the behavior and emotional well-being that appear ubiquitously both within and outside of Christianity? I don't know if individuals are born with greater genetic predispositions toward empathy or selflessness, if they had exceptional parenting, or experienced extraordinary circumstances in their lives. It may be several years or several generations before we understand why or how some individuals are gifted with more of these desirable characteristics than others, but any connection to Christianity or the acceptance and pursuit of the Christian god, seems more coincidental than causal. Muslims, Jews, Atheists, Satanists, Buddhists, and Hindus manifest the full array of these traits, so while the origins of morality and joy are still philosophically inconclusive, these traits do not appear to come exclusively from a belief in and personal relationship with the Christian god.

And what about the less desirable qualities most of us are trying to discard from our lives, such as excessive selfishness, worrying, and greed? I still see depression, anxiety, hate, deviancy, rape, and child abuse within Christianity at no lesser occurrence than outside of Christianity. Given this reality, how can Christianity be advertised as a remedy for any of these attributes and behaviors?

I believed drawing close to Christ changes people, and further that those changes are evidence that Christianity works. But when it didn't work, or when there was no lasting change, I never turned a critical eye toward Christianity, just the Christian – the person must be to blame. I was convinced that the overwhelming number of Christians who still excessively worry either aren't praying enough or aren't praying correctly. Either they aren't reading the Bible enough or they aren't reading it correctly. Either they need to look at their circumstances differently, listen differently to the still small voice, have more faith, or make any number of other tweaks to their spiritual walk. New books continue to be written, all telling Christians the answer to their problems is just more faith or one changed perspective away.

I have not observed that doing more Christian things, and believing more, will result in the kind of lasting change I seek. If I had seen that Christianity was uniquely less impacted by these character and personality traits, or if Christians were happier, or more at peace, then a stronger case could be made for the influence of Christianity on people's lives.

But I had repeatedly seen people's lives improve, at least temporarily, after accepting Christ. I have seen the story of Jesus dying on the cross have an immediate impact on the way people feel about themselves, and I've seen it start them on a path toward self-improvement. But again, Christianity is not unique in this way, and if Christ is to be credited for changing these lives, then all other religions and gods must be credited for similar changes in the lives of their believers. We must credit the Hindu gods for all the good done by Hindus and the positive changes in their lives, and we must credit Zoroastrian gods for the good done by their believers.

Because the Christian god cannot be seen, his impact on the lives of those who seek and love him *could* prove to be an effective witness for his power. It would speak volumes about the value of Christianity if Christians exhibited more joy, peace, and hope than worshipers of other gods and deniers of all gods. Christianity would be a more credible source for morality if Christians exhibited any homogeneity in moral convictions. I firmly believe that if a group has faith in and routinely solicits an all-knowing and all-powerful god or set of gods, and everyone else either solicits imaginary gods or does not pray at all, there should be observable differences in the lives of those who are connected to real power and real knowledge. Christians exhibit no such differences, and if there are no differences then I fail to see the value.

Agnostic Atheism

If I was no longer Christian, what was I? "Atheist" initially sounded like a hurtful curse word to me, so it felt better to call myself agnostic, which most people understand to be questioning. I've since learned that agnosticism and atheism aren't what I thought they were, and I'm an agnostic Atheist. Agnosticism and Gnosticism refer to what a person thinks can be known, in this case about a supernatural god. Atheism and theism refer to whether a person believes a supernatural god exists. As a shorthand, these terms can be combined and understood in the following ways:

Agnostic Atheist – doubts the existence of God
Gnostic Atheist – is certain God does not exist

Agnostic Theist – believes God likely exists
Gnostic Theist – is certain God exists

I don't believe the existence or nonexistence of a supernatural being can ever be proven beyond a shadow of a doubt. The writer Arthur Clarke suggested that "any sufficiently advanced technology is indistinguishable from magic." This is to say that advanced technology can appear supernatural. Just imagine someone from the 1700s witnessing a video call, or someone wielding a gun 2,000 years ago – the technology would seem supernatural. And now, there may be advanced civilizations elsewhere in our universe. So, even if apparently supernatural events were an established part of our lives, we could not eliminate the possibility that this is just advanced technology being perpetrated on us.

The theory I love best is that our entire universe is an alien child's middle school science project, the way our children build ant farms. So, even if there were burning bushes and bodies of water being divided into two, this could all be the work of a curious child. Of course, there is no evidence for this, and we can never know, hence my agnosticism.

At some point, it may be more useful to believe we are all here because of a creator god, rather than a petulant alien child. As of right now though, there simply isn't enough evidence to support my belief in a supernatural god, and further that he is mingling in the affairs of humans. Because of this belief, or lack thereof, I am an Atheist. Again, I cannot prove the Christian god doesn't exist, but I do not believe he does, and I live my life accordingly.

The stereotype most Christians seem to have of atheists is that they are all gnostic atheists, meaning they claim to know for sure there is no God. This may be a reaction to the arrogance many atheists convey when discussing their perspective on the matter, but nearly all the atheists I know believe the existence or non-existence of God cannot be known, but that the evidence for God falls short of making it a likely reality. So, we choose to live as if there is no god.

I do not have even an anecdotal guess for the ratio of gnostic theists to agnostic theists within Christianity. The gnostic theists are certain of God's existence beyond a shadow of a doubt, and the agnostic theists claim that although the existence of God cannot be known, it is either likely or useful enough for them to believe he does.

I have encountered the most friction with gnostic theists, of course. As an agnostic atheist, gnostic theism represents the opposite ends of both spectrums. The friction arises from the assertion that what is to be known about God and his will is easily discoverable. This is not to say gnostic theists believe being a Christian is easy, but that the existence of God is easily observable and apparent in nature, Bibles, archeology, and often even science. It is typically obvious to them in a way that makes my not seeing God somewhat incomprehensible. So, then there is the presumption that I'm choosing not to see God, or that I do not want to see God. Or worse, that I see God but am rejecting him to be obtuse or selfish in some way. I have repeatedly heard these rationalizations for my lack of belief, and I understand them completely. If an object was obviously visible to me, and a friend could see everything in a scene except that object, I too would wonder what sort of game they're playing. That said, most gnostic theists will find almost zero value in this book.

I prefer to simply call myself an Atheist, rather than agnostic, because it better describes the way I live my life regarding spirituality. But I would much rather describe myself as a scientist, non-vegetarian, humanist, and silly father – long before I mention my Atheism.

Are you gnostic or agnostic? Are you an atheist or a theist? Perhaps you're a deist, a pandeist, or an apatheist.

Chapter 10

My Alternative

So, what *do* I believe in now? What guides my moral compass? How do I explain and endure suffering? What is the meaning of life?

It's quite easy for me to be critical of Christianity or any other belief system for their answers to these questions, but leaving Christianity inspired me to seek out new answers to these and other questions, and to hold my new answers to a similarly high level of scrutiny. All de-converted Christians do not do this – some choose to answer different questions, or none at all. But here are a few of the questions I've heard the most since leaving Christianity and feel compelled to answer.

Haven't I ever felt the presence of God?

On a couple occasions, yes, I absolutely felt what I thought was the presence of God. My body felt warm and my mind felt comforted and reassured, but I now attribute those feelings to other causes. I had been told for many years what the presence of God feels like, so when I felt those things, it was easy to accept that God wanted me to feel his presence.

I now recognize that our vision, hearing, imagination, feelings, hopes, and memories can alter our perception of an experience to fit a preconceived narrative, such as the superiority of our own gender or race, the purity of our own actions, or the presence of an invisible deity I've been told about my whole life. Our senses can be manipulated by the expectations and desires of our subconscious minds. Any Christian who thinks this isn't possible expresses a fundamental misunderstanding about how the human mind works, and must explain the experiences of billions of people, both past and present, who have interacted with non-Christian gods.

Members of all theology-based religions share these experiences, so Christianity is not unique in this way. And the explanations Christians use to disregard other people's experiences with non-Christian gods apply similarly to my own prior experiences with the Christian god.

How do I determine right from wrong?

It isn't clear that Christians do better at "right and wrong" than non-Christians, and there has always been disagreement among Christians about what they should and shouldn't do. I often turn the question back to the asker, but this is genuinely something everyone should spend time thinking through. I also have children and feel a deep responsibility to teach them the basics of right and wrong, despite what some believe is an innate sense of morality we are born with.

It should be noted that no source of morality is exact or completely thorough. Christianity does not provide direct guidance for every situation a person might find themselves in, and neither should it be expected to. The best any moral framework can do is to provide a set of principles from which to draw upon.

My moral compass is centered around compassion, kindness, empathy, equality, integrity, generosity, and self-determination. I am probably forgetting a couple other ideas, and these are just a generic set of principles. Among other things, I must think carefully about how equality should look, how to be generous in meaningful ways, and how to provide thoughtful and non-reactive honesty. When facing real-life situations that involve moral nuance and layered complexity, I must extract from these ideas specific behaviors and desired outcomes.

I also integrate the idea of balance into my moral landscape. I seek to balance my own needs and desires with the needs and desires of others. In pursuit of my own joy, love, comfort, and peace, and in pursuit of those things for the people I love, I must consider the impact of my decisions on other people and take responsibility for them. To better achieve my own goals, and to recognize more clearly how others are affected, I must strive to understand what is most likely true about myself, my actions, and their consequences.

None of the above has changed from when I left Christianity. My parents, through the lens of their own faith, set me up with a moral foundation that included all the above. But as I've encountered the world, the process by which Christians pursue morality became problematic because of its dependence on a 2,000-year-old book and interaction with an invisible god. I saw subjectivity as a significant stumbling block to the process of understanding what is right or good. Each individual's perspective of the world is narrow, and our perception of things is not always accurate or even useful. This makes the collective intelligence, perspective, and contribution of many diverse observers necessary to best understand what behaviors and outcomes are more moral than others. To achieve balance, I must seek perspectives different than my own, and different than those of my family, friends, immediate community, and even countrymen.

I do believe the Bible has good counsel, as does the Quran and other ancient books, Shakespeare's Othello, Michael Jackson's Man in the Mirror, and many other works of art on the nature of humanity. Many Christians agree with this and are not so narrowly focused on religious texts that they can't see the good in other sources. But I no longer privilege the Christian texts, which means I do not intentionally start or end any pursuit of moral guidance with the Bible. Nor do I

119

allow it to trump other sources. I do not listen for the still small voice of God to explain what is more right or more wrong about certain plans of action. I try to read indiscriminately to learn about other cultures and walks of life, and I often seek opportunities to meet and listen to people from different backgrounds. I am constantly trying to fit new ideas and understandings of our humanity into a model of how I should interact in the world, and I must never stop working to find better balance.

How do I endure suffering?

My mother is perhaps most curious about this. Without teaching my children the value of a relationship with Jesus Christ, she asked how I will equip them to cope in a world that is often very cold and unforgiving? Sickness, unexpected death, job loss, and broken relationships are all things most people can look forward to experiencing throughout their lives, and my mother views her Christianity as a dam against the emotional load that can accompany life's setbacks.

History has taught me two valuable lessons about suffering. First, it will happen. No one is immune. Kings, paupers, saints, and the kindest and most gentle souls to ever live – they've all suffered. The second lesson is that we can carry on. Our minds adapt and negotiate through all sorts of tragedies. There are people right now enduring and overcoming unimaginable circumstances, and we can learn about our own strength by recognizing the strength in others.

When we only deeply connect with Christians, however, and only listen to the struggles and victories of other Christians, it's easy to believe that overcoming is exclusive to Christianity. But just as suffering occurs indiscriminately, people of all walks of life, all religions, and even Atheists make it through difficult times, and sometimes smile throughout the journey. It's hard to believe I need a relationship with Jesus Christ when so many people without this relationship are persevering and overcoming. It seems more likely that what we need to endure suffering is already inside each of us, and accessible to everyone, instead of only those who seek Christ.

Many people find the strength to overcome in family and friends, in their purpose, and what appears to be a basic human desire not to give up. I am interested in understanding and fostering these sources of strength and learning how to best support the people around me who may need it.

What is the origin of the universe? How did we get here?

I don't know. Young Earth creationists hold that the Earth was created, or at least populated, approximately six thousand years ago, but this and other intelligent design hypotheses aren't supported by what we observe in the natural world.

Looking at the universe with great awe and wonder isn't evidence that it must have been created. I have been accused of rejecting Christianity because it can't answer all of life's questions, but at best Science also has only an educated guess, albeit based on more observable facts. And although I am very curious about this question, I can still be a good father, friend, and teacher without an exact answer.

What happens after death?

Our bodies begin to decompose shortly after death, and the molecules and energy we are comprised of disperse to become parts of other systems and organisms. Perhaps in the future there will be evidence of souls leaving the body to return to heaven or linger in purgatory, but for now, I don't see any benefit in accepting this belief on the premise of faith.

I no longer believe the Earth is just our temporary home, and that we are passing through on our way to heaven. We may eventually find other habitable planets, but this Earth will be our home for the foreseeable future. Accepting this, I now feel more obligated to take care of the planet for future generations.

I am more motivated to spend time with my close friends and family now, because I don't anticipate having an eternity with them in the afterlife. I want my children to spend time with their grandparents, aunts, and uncles, learning valuable family history and life lessons, as was passed to me by family members who have gone before. I cherish their memories and contributions to my life and hope to honor them by the way I live in *this* life.

What is my purpose?

Finding one's purpose can be extremely rewarding since it can provide some focus for the tasks we decide to take on, and can make the struggles of life seem more worthwhile. I was still attending church a few years ago when the Christian-authored book "The Purpose Driven Life" was released. Its worldwide success showed that many Christians were struggling to identify their purpose. This is to say that both inside and outside of Christianity, finding one's purpose can be very challenging.

Less-complex animals go about their lives executing on a clear purpose without self-help books and discussions on existential philosophy. By being such a complex species, though, humans can take on an innumerable number of tasks, so choosing exactly which of these things we should be doing can be daunting. In trying to keep things simple, my purpose is derived from an understanding of my individual strengths and opportunities. What am I good at? What resources are available to me? What tasks need to be done?

Currently, I have multiple purposes. I am an Engineering professor, and I want to encourage my students to think more about their social responsibility as young engineers. I also feel compelled to teach people in my community about the benefit of using scientific inquiry in their everyday lives. Writing this letter and turning it into a book has been driven by that purpose. I am also a parent, and I want my children to become productive and compassionate global citizens.

Many of us think our lives should have a singular purpose, and that we were born to do one thing or to pursue one goal. But our lives change, and we can seek out new purposes in each stage. A purpose can last a lifetime but may be as short as a moment. I try to think about the world I want to live in, and then pursue an activity that pushes us, even a little bit, toward that goal.

What hope do I have?

It's difficult to compete with heaven. What's better than seeing all the people you've ever loved and lost, and spending an eternity laughing and singing and flying from galaxy to galaxy with them? There's gold and silver and crowns and mansions. Other faith systems offer virgins or nirvana, but they all come with a catch – you must die before receiving the reward. Or the world must be destroyed, whichever one comes first.

Bibles predicted the world would come to an end "soon," but these texts were written thousands of years ago. Even when I was a Christian, I wasn't motivated by the confounding interpretation of *soon* by which the next thing I would experience after death is the resurrection and second coming of Jesus Christ, so it's "soon" for me. Promises about the afterlife failed to inspire me because they can never be corroborated, even if another 2,000 years go by. It seems like the hallmark of any good faith-based religion is the promise of things in the afterlife because those types of claims can never be challenged.

Afterlife narratives also fail to help solve problems here on Earth. The story of Christianity teaches an ever-diminishing stature and character of humanity, so although some Christians do not believe in the literal Adam character, they believe humans as a species, and our society as a whole, are getting worse, and that our only redemption will come through the second coming of Jesus Christ. I was told that the Christian god will only destroy the world and rebuild it after we've all devolved into a nearly irredeemable mess.

On the contrary, I believe my children can help to create a world better than the one they were born into. There will always be setbacks and compromises, but women are now more integrated into political and professional life than they've ever been, democracies are replacing autocracies around the world, illiteracy rates are dropping, and more people have access to higher levels of education than ever before. Things on Earth can get better, and this potential progress is the source of my hope.

But I will admit that things look daunting. With so much seemingly random suffering in the world, so much greed and selfishness, and no answer for misinformation, I'm not super optimistic about where humanity is headed. Sorry...

What is the meaning of life?

I don't know, but I don't think we need to know the meaning of life to find meaning *in* life.

Am I just replacing my faith in God with a faith in science?

Science is not simply a compiled list of established facts to be believed – it's a method for subjecting the things we believe to a reality check. For better or worse, humans are very gullible and tend to believe what makes us feel good or what confirms a previously held belief, and science forces us to reconcile our beliefs with what is known about the world as observed through more objective lenses.

More objective observations have a long history of providing more reliable understandings of things when compared to less objective observations. This is largely due to our subjective biases and limited perspective of the world. The reliance of Christianity on personal faith makes it practically antithetical to the desire for objectivity, so my move away from Christianity is the result of shifting confidence away from my own subjectivity, and toward collective objectivity.

Yes, I have accepted scientific findings without personally doing the experiments. And yes, this can constitute as faith. So, then yes, I do have more faith in the process of science than the process of Christianity. But I see a significant difference between the belief in ideas based on experiments I could run, and believing in things for which no experiment can verify.

I can also accept things to be likely true without the existence of absolute proof. Adhering to the tenets of scientific inquiry doesn't require explicit proof before believing or acting on information. This is a misunderstanding of science. Instead, Science seeks to put forward the best available explanation, using the best available information, which has been gathered in the best available way. So, even without explicit proof, I prefer explanations based on evidence, and data gathered through experimentation.

Can't faith in God co-exist with my appreciation for scientific inquiry?

Christianity isn't just about the love of God. It also makes suggestions about *how* to think about evidence, facts, and feelings. My parents and most of my family practice a very moderate and loving iteration of Christianity, but buried under layers of warm hugs and family worships are some very dangerous ideas – that we will not always understand why we are to do certain things, that we should believe things even when faced with evidence to the contrary, and that we will receive our reward in the afterlife. I simply cannot abide by these problematic ideas anymore.

I have heard that Science can tell us *what* we are, but not *why* we are, and that there are other big questions Science just cannot answer. These have always been the justifications for faith-based beliefs to co-exist with scientific inquiry, but I am confident we can have ethical and fulfilling lives without needing to accept things solely based on faith, and without the availability of direct evidence. I do not object to anyone's desire to wonder about the supernatural, and I stand in awe of how much humanity does not know about the universe, but I cannot accept any philosophy which suggests the *need* to believe in one particular narrative about this unknown, and to support this belief by faith. I no longer believe I need Jesus to have peace and happiness, or that I need to get into the Christian's idea of heaven.

On the other hand, I believe we need more objectivity, more reason, and more evidence-based decision making in all aspects of society. This is why I am glad to be alive in the era of science, and why I choose to advocate passionately for evidence over faith.

HOW-ish Sermon

I had already written most of this book and settled into my atheism before I came across a sermon by Rev. Dr. Howard-John Wesley on YouTube. Yes, I still enjoy good oration on a topic I still care deeply about (and I still listen to gospel music). The sermon, titled "The Bible Says...", was part of a Come As You Are (C.A.Y.A.) series and aired on May 1, 2019. That should be enough information to find the video on YouTube, if desired.

I've heard thousands of sermons in my life, but this was the only one that seriously explored the question: "How do you know God?" There's the key word: How. Wesley acknowledged that while many old-school Christians claim that knowledge of God comes solely from the Bible, scripture can be interpreted in conflicting ways, so "The Bible says…" cannot be a person's only guiding light. He suggested that believers actually rely on six sources:

1. Scripture (Bible)
2. Inspiration (Holy Spirit)
3. Intellect/Reason (Theology)
4. Tradition (Church)
5. Personal Experience (Testimony)
6. Nature (Creation)

Wesley encouraged people to rank these methods according to how they apply in their own lives, and when sources come into conflict, higher-ranked tools should overrule lower-ranked ones. He then presented his own personal ranking: Scripture (25%), Experience (25%), Inspiration (17.5%), Intellect (17.5%), Tradition (10%), and Nature (5%). And he noted that as he's aged, he's had more experiences with God so that has taken on a greater role, while scripture once had a stronger influence.

After preaching for an hour, Wesley ended the sermon and promised to finish it the next month, but he never did, and no explanation was given. The sermon received mixed reactions in the comments. Some praised its nuance, while others criticized the idea that anything could take precedence over the Bible.

Maybe it's fitting that the sermon never continued. It doesn't feel like Christianity ever truly resolves the nuances of *how* believers are supposed to know God. Each person is then left to figure it out on their own, using tools that are vulnerable to subjective bias and experiences that are deeply personal and often conflicting.

Wesley came closer than most preachers to acknowledging the deeply subjective nature of Christianity's *how*, even if he stopped short of questioning the validity of the tools themselves. Despite my deconversion, I still find these conversations fascinating. And this sermon reinforced what I had already come to realize – there is no reliable or even near-objective way to know God. But if more Christians wrestled with these questions, maybe Christian practice would look very different.

If you were to create your own ranking of tools for determining truth – not just in religion, but in any area – what would it look like?

Chapter 11

The Appeal

(When I was a child, most of the good sermons ended with an appeal. An organist or pianist played softly while the preacher made an emotional plea for the congregants to make a decision for Christ, or to rededicate themselves to living more Christlike. Sometimes this included a commitment to be baptized, but more often individuals were asked to leave their seats and come down to the front of the church for special prayer. I don't have soft music or a prayer to offer, but this is my appeal to you nonetheless.)

I have been told a few times that Science cannot explain everything, and that a thing not being measurable isn't an indication that it isn't real or doesn't exist. But I already agree with these statements and the sentiment behind them. Things are happening to and around us that we cannot currently measure and may not be able to measure for many years. So, people have claimed to learn about some of these immeasurable realities through visions, dreams, inspired texts, isolated incidents, solitary experiences, feelings, intuition, impressions, inspiration, mysterious occurrences, decoded prophecies, and a host of other unrepeatable or unverifiable experiences. But these kinds of tools and processes are problematic because our interpretations of our experiences are incomplete due to our limited perspective and are skewed because of our biases.

These problematic tools and processes are informed by what people believe to be irrefutable experiences, which makes them difficult to challenge and correct any misunderstandings or misperceptions. The pathways back to unaltered reality and truth are severed by self-confidence, leaving individuals feeling empowered to develop ideas and beliefs about the world based on information that may be severely errant. These are the kinds of experiences Christianity is built on, and our subjective perspective of those experiences is the sinking sand at the foundation of Christian faith. This is not to say everything Christians believe is false, but what Christians believe has risen out of processes that are dangerously susceptible to our traditions, desires, fears, and expectations.

If worshipers of the one true god, who is omnipotent, omnipresent, and omniscient, do not exhibit appreciably different lives than worshipers of false gods and deniers of all gods, my only guess is that this god isn't communicating effectively with his believers. If an invisible, inaudible, and intangible god exists, but has only made himself accessible through personal and unverifiable experiences, he will most certainly be widely misunderstood and misused. His decision to be inconspicuous inevitably leads to a great deal of pain and suffering at the hands of people who believe they have communicated with him but haven't. Those of us who are gullible and impressionable do not stand a chance, but we are all gullible and impressionable. Truth cannot be reliably discerned through these processes, facts cannot be verified, and disagreements cannot be settled between two individuals who both claim to have heard from God. If this nebulous plan is the best the Christian god can do, then I'm uninterested in him, even if he is real.

Many people who walk away from Christianity do not distill their objections down to the root cause, as I have tried to do here, but they likely recognize a pervasive ugliness in Christianity. I used to accept this as an artifact of any human-centered institution. I believed the flaw was in humanity, not Christianity. But Christianity and other faith-based belief systems offer no resistance to the problematic aspects of our psyches that cause all the ugliness. Maybe there are ways to interpret the Bible, understand prophecy, and communicate with God that aren't so vulnerable to our subjectivity, but those processes can only be pursued after the limitations of the current approaches are acknowledged. And in the 2,000 years of Christianity, I'm not aware of any substantive discussion about this need.

Instead, Christianity proceeds through the employ of tools we as humans innately cannot be successful using – at least not at the scale Christians suggest we can be. In Christianity, every person is to hear from God, which is to claim that every person can discern supernatural thoughts from their own thoughts. In Christianity, every person is to interpret the Bible, which is to say that every person can understand what versions and verses God protected, and which ones he didn't. This is also to say that every person can know which texts God is speaking to all people for all time, and which texts Paul, for instance, is only speaking to the addressees of his letters. In Christianity, every person should recognize signs and miracles, which is to say that every person can know when an invisible god has moved, and is able to distinguish that from the results of natural physical laws, some of which we aren't even aware of yet.

These are dangerous claims to make about our abilities to effectively use such vulnerable processes, and thousands of years of written human history show us in painful detail how bad things can get when individuals mistake their perception for reality, and then construct communities and belief systems based on what is ultimately not true. In the context of belief building, we should be using history to better understand how our desires, fears, preconceived notions, and other subjective influences impact our perception and experiences. Even the processes of observations and testable hypotheses are not immune to the influence of personal bias. We are still learning how fragile our senses are, and how persuadable we are to propaganda and indoctrination, and we must continuously incorporate new information about ourselves into the processes we use to understand what is real and what is true.

We owe it to our ancestors to do this, and to build better belief systems with the knowledge we've gained about ourselves from their stories. Because our relationships benefit from more accurate understandings of each other, and our communities are stronger and can benefit more people when they are organized around ideas that most closely represent reality. Before we get into any debates about *what* we believe – what the nature of humanity is, what the origins of Earth are, what happens after we die, what the roles of women are, what our relationship to nature should be, what homosexuals should and shouldn't be doing – we need to be critical of *how* we came to these beliefs, and *how* our beliefs should be shaped going forward.

We owe it to the women who were burned at the stake because of witchcraft allegations. We owe it to the deaf, dumb, and otherwise ill who were subjected to obscene and ineffective treatments because of isolated success stories. We owe it to enslaved Americans whose bondage was justified by the "scientific" understanding and general feeling that Blacks and Whites were two different species. Continuing to empower the same vulnerable and ineffective tools and processes that brought us these and countless other tragedies would be a mockery to the struggles of these people, and it doesn't have to be this way.

We must temper our enthusiasm for understanding and new insight with humility toward our own ability to see, hear, and experience the world as it really is. We must do the hard work of seeking more objective perspectives when they are available and prioritize them over our more subjective experiences and intuitions.

We must forever remain in pursuit of a better *how* – one that evolves with our understanding of ourselves, embraces correction, can be practiced correctly by more and more people, and becomes increasingly helpful in our daily lives as we refine it.

Quotes

1. You can safely assume you've created God in your own image when it turns out that God hates all the same people you do.

    - Anne Lamott

2. Tell me the reasons you don't believe in all the other gods, and those are the reasons I don't believe in yours.

    - Unknown

3. Selling eternal life is an unbeatable business, with no customers asking for their money back after the goods are not delivered.

    - Victor J. Stenger

4. It's easier to fool people than convince them that they've been fooled.

    - Unknown

5. Isn't this enough?
   Just this world?
   Just this beautiful, complex, wonderfully unfathomable, natural world?
   How does it so fail to hold our attention that we have to diminish it with the invention of cheap, man-made myths and monsters?

   - Tim Minchin, "Storm"

6. Science truths transcend personal belief systems.

   - Neil deGrasse Tyson

7. People generally see what they look for and hear what they listen for.

   - Judge Taylor in Harper Lee's "To Kill a Mockingbird"

8. Doubt is the great fuel of all inquiry, of all discovery, and of all innovation.

   - Christopher Hitchens

9. Time makes ancient good uncouth.

    - James Russell Lowell

10. All religions, arts, and sciences are branches of the same tree. All these aspirations are directed toward enabling man's life, lifting it from the sphere of mere physical existence and leading the individual towards freedom.

    - Albert Einstein

11. You can't believe everything you think.

    - Unknown

12. When a claim is falsified in science, everyone agrees it is bogus, it's discarded and put into the trash bin of bad ideas. When a claim is falsified in religion, it becomes a metaphor.

    - Jerry Coyne

13. Those people who leap from personal bafflement of a natural phenomenon straight to a hasty invocation of the supernatural are no better than the fools who see a conjurer bending a spoon and leap to the conclusion that it is paranormal.

    - Richard Dawkins

14. Organized belief systems which fail to adapt to changing mores are demoted from religions to acknowledged metaphoric myth systems. No one worships Odin anymore, or Zeus.

    - Temperance "Bones" Brennan on the TV Show "Bones," Season 2, Episode 17, written by Lyla Oliver

15. A wise man proportions his belief to the evidence.

    - David Hume

16. If science proves some belief of Buddhism wrong, then Buddhism will have to change.

    - The 14th Dalai Lama

17. It ain't what you don't know that gets you in trouble. It's what you know for sure that just ain't so.

    - Mark Twain

18. The most dangerous people in the world are the ones who have God all figured out with absolute certainty.

    - Howard-John Wesley

19. Truth is like poetry. And most people hate poetry.

    - Unknown

20. The less people know, the more stubbornly they know it.

    - Rajneesh (Osho)

21. Everything happens for a reason. That reason is physics.

    - Unknown

22. Christianity's power comes from its malleability.

    - Reza Aslim

23. Lots of things happen after you die – they just don't involve you.

    - Unknown

24. I know of no society in recorded history that suffered because its people became too reasonable.

    - Sam Harris

25. I don't think that God exists. I think that makes the most sense of the evidence that I have and my experience.

    - Ryan Bell

26. Those who believe without reason cannot be convinced with reason.

    - James Randi

27. I wish there were a beautiful building where I could ritualize the transitions in my life, and in my daughter's life, with great music, and with great art, but where what we know about the world is not blatantly ignored.

    - Julia Sweeney

28. The invisible and the nonexistent often look a lot alike.

    - Banning McKown

29. I would request that my body in death be buried not cremated, so that the energy content contained within it gets returned to the earth, so that flora and fauna can dine upon it, just as I have dined upon flora and fauna during my lifetime.

    - Neil deGrasse Tyson

30. I would rather have questions that can't be answered than answers that can't be questioned.

    - Richard Feynman

31. As the area of our knowledge grows, so too does the perimeter of our ignorance.

    - Neil deGrasse Tyson

32. I contend that we are both atheists. I just believe in one fewer god than you do. When you understand why you dismiss all the other possible gods, you will understand why I dismiss yours.

- Stephen Robert

33. It's his autobiography. He wrote it! Of course he made himself look like the hero.

- Lucifer

34. If it turns out there is a God, I don't think that he's evil. But the worst that you can say about him is that basically he's an underachiever.

- Woody Allen

35. What can be accepted without evidence can also be dismissed without evidence.

- Christopher Hitchens

36. Say what you will about the sweet miracle of unquestioning faith; I consider a capacity for it terrifying and absolutely vile.

    - Kurt Vonnegut

37. The church says the earth is flat, but I know that it is round, for I have seen the shadow on the moon, and I have more faith in a shadow than in the church.

    - Ferdinand Magellan

38. Extraordinary claims require extraordinary evidence.

    - Carl Sagan

39. Why should I allow that same God to tell me how to raise my kids, who had to drown His own?

    - Robert G. Ingersoll

40. Sin is an imaginary disease, invented to sell you an imaginary cure.

    - Unknown

41. Religion is regarded by the common people as true, by the wise as false, and by the rulers as useful.

    - Edward Gibbon

42. It's an incredible con job when you think about it, to believe something now in exchange for something after death. Even corporations with their reward systems don't try to make it posthumous.

    - Gloria Steinem

43. The reason to be an atheist is not that it makes us feel better or gives us a more rewarding life. The reason to be an atheist is simply that there is no God, and we would prefer to live in full recognition of that, accepting the consequences, even if it makes us less happy.

    - Julian Baggini

44. Yes, I do have proof that God does not exist.
It is perfect and irrefutable.
I'm not going to show it to you, however.
You cannot see it or detect it in any way.
You cannot deduct it from the laws of logic either.
You might claim that I do in fact have no such proof.
But you have no proof that I don't.
Sound familiar?

- Rune Friberg

45. If we take any fiction, and any holy book, and destroy it, in a thousand years' time, that wouldn't come back just as it was. Whereas if we took every science book, and every fact, and destroyed them all, in a thousand years, they would all be back. Because all the same tests would be the same result. So, I don't need faith in science.

- Ricky Gervais

46. Properly read, the Bible is the most potent force for atheism ever conceived.

- Isaac Asimov

47. Being a Humanist means trying to behave decently without expectation of rewards or punishment after you are dead.

   -   Kurt Vonnegut

48. May the sanctity of your knowledge be corrupted by insight.

   -   Unknown

49. What I'm asking you to entertain is that there is nothing we need to believe on insufficient evidence to have deeply ethical and spiritual lives.

   -   Sam Harris

50. I don't think it is good mental health practice to fantasize that you know the infinite thoughts of imaginary entities.

   -   Stefan Molyneux

51. HEAVEN: The big apartheid in the sky.

   -   Philip Appleman

52. You either have a God who sends child rapists to rape children or you have a God who simply watches it and says, 'When you're done, I'm going to punish you.' If I could stop a person from raping a child, I would. That's the difference between me and your God.

    - Tracie Harris

53. If by some bizarre chance there turns out to be a god [...], I'm willing to bet he's an atheist too.

    - Salman Rushdie

54. Believe those who are seeking the truth. Doubt those who find it.

    - André Gide

55. When I die...
    My body stops functioning
    Shuts down
    All at once, or gradually
    My breathing stops, by heart stops beating – clinical death
    And a bit later, like 5 whole minutes later,
    my brain cells start dying
    But in the meantime, in between, maybe my brain releases a flood of DMT

It's the psychedelic drug released when we dream, so...
I dream
I dream bigger than I have ever dreamed before because
it's all of it
Just the last dump of DMT all at once
And my neurons are firing and I'm seeing this firework
display of memories and imagination
And I am just tripping
I mean, really tripping balls because my mind's rifling
through the memories
You know, the long and short-term, and the dreams mix
with the memories, and...
It's a curtain call
The dream to end all dreams
One last great dream as my mind empties the fuckin'
missile silos and then...
I stop
My brain activity ceases and there is nothing left of me
No pain
No memory
No awareness that I ever was
Everything is as it was before me
And the electricity disperses from my brain until it's just
dead tissue
Meat
Oblivion
And all the other little things that make me up,

the microbes, and the billion other little things that live
on my eyelashes
and in my hair and in my mouth and on my skin
and in my gut and everywhere else...
they just keep on living...
and eating
And I'm serving a purpose
I'm feeding life
And I'm broken apart and all the littlest pieces of me are
just recycled
And I'm billions of other places
And my atoms are in plants and bugs and animals
And I am like the stars that are in the sky
There one moment and then just scattered across the
goddamn cosmos.

- Riley Flynn from the TV Show "Midnight
  Mass," Season 1, Episode 5, written by Mike
  Flanagan and James Flanagan